MARINE SURVEYS

AN INTRODUCTION

By
C. F. DURHAM

Master Mariner, F.R. Met. S.,
Member Company of Master Mariners
of Australia, A.M.A.I.M. M.N.I.

Fairplay Publications

Published and distributed by
FAIRPLAY PUBLICATIONS LTD
52/54 Southwark Street, London SE1 1UJ
Telephone 403 3164
Telex 884595 FPLAY G

ISBN 0 905045 33 5

Typeset by JJ Typographics Ltd., Rochford, Essex.
Printed by Mayhew McCrimmon Printers Ltd., Gt. Wakering, Essex.

THE AUTHOR

C. F. Durham served afloat in both cargo and passenger ships of the P&O, reaching the rank of Chief Officer before he came ashore as Assistant Harbour Master in Nauru. He then moved to the new port of Weipa in Australia as Marine and General Transport Superintendent, with responsibilities that ranged from surveying to pilotage and stevedoring, ship's agency to the building and crewing of the tug fleet. After a spell relieving in command of one of the world's biggest salvage tugs based in South Africa, he became the representative at Richards Bay of the Société Générale de Surveillance, where much of this book was written.

Preface

The marine surveyor occupies a special place in the marine industry, although strangely there is not a great deal published about his work. The mariner knows him by reputation, when he appears at the opening of hatches, or patiently asking questions after damage has been reported. The cargo owner, or the cargo insurer who employs the surveyor sees the end product of his work, which is what he is judged by, although exactly how he arrives at his conclusions may not be known.

This book is an introduction to the work of the marine surveyor and it is hoped that it will be of interest to both those professionals perhaps contemplating a career as a marine surveyor, those who are in training, and perhaps more importantly, the enormous numbers of people who employ marine surveyors.

The front cover photograph was kindly supplied by Aalborg Marine Limited, London.

Contents

Introduction

The Marine Surveyor can be called on to do a number of different surveys, and this book, which is not an exhaustive study of what is, a very large subject, has been written with the object of offering general guidance to those who may be required to carry out surveys, or require them to be carried out.

Most of the surveys that may be required can be reduced to four basic types.

(a) Determining the quantity of cargo loaded or discharged from a ship.

(b) To establish the condition of the hull and/or equipment.

(c) To establish fairly the degree of damage to cargo equipment, or hull and, if possible to establish the cause of the loss or damage or to check that work or repairs have been carried out as required.

(d) To determine the suitability of a compartment or equipment for a specific cargo or that cargo has been loaded to specific requirements.

But all have common factors — viz.

(i) that the successful completion of the survey is dependent upon the experience, efficiency and integrity of the surveyor and

(ii) that the survey report must be written dispassionately and in such a way that the complete picture is given.

Should a surveyor find himself in the position, where because of the nature of any condition or the type of damage, or because of his unfamiliarity with any commodity, he is not qualified to express an authorative opinion, he should immediately consult someone who has the necessary knowledge. The person consulted must be independent, and of such standing that his findings are unlikely to be questioned. The employment of such an expert in no way reflects upon the ability of a surveyor, and usually the inclusion of an expert's findings in a surveyor's report enhances the value of such a report.

Sometimes, the survey to be done is covered by statutory regulations, as for example, in the case of grain cargoes, or damage to the hull, and Government or Class surveyors may also be in attendance. Although it is usually the responsibility of these surveyors to determine whether the ship meets the statutory regulations or class requirements, it does not absolve the independent Marine Surveyor from his duty of conducting his survey and making his report to those who commissioned him, as though the responsibility were his.

The Survey Report

The importance of drafting this document properly cannot be too strongly emphasised, as if the wording is not correct, an alteration to the existing condition of the cargo, equipment or hull, can be implied, and the liability for any damage, now or in the future, shifted from one party to another, or even to the surveyor himself. Often, especially in the case of a damage survey, it is the only evidence that underwriters and others, usually far from the site of the survey, have to determine the extent of their liability.

The report should contain as far as possible, only statements of fact, and any opinions expressed should be able to be substantiated by factual information. All relevant information must be detailed, including an history of the movement of any cargo involved, or the events leading up to, and after any accident, and any relevant log entries.

In the case of cargo, the report should contain details of the total consignment, giving marks and numbers etc. and how many items were found damaged and how many in good condition, detailing the damage found in each of the damaged items. It should also contain the time and date that notification was given to the carrier or carriers.

Pictures often speak louder than words, and photographs, drawings or sketches are a definite asset to any survey report.

The survey report belongs to the person commissioning that report and the surveyor is not at liberty to show or give the report to another party without the express approval of the person commissioning the report.

Qualifications

It is odd, in this world, where specialisation is a fetish, that there is no requisite qualification, or even a Society to set standards for a Marine Surveyor. All that is required is that the man doing the survey is acceptable to the parties concerned with the results of the survey. In order to be so acceptable, it us usual, but not mandatory for the surveyor to have a Master Mariners', or Chief Engineer's Certificate, or be a qualified Naval Architect or Boat Builder. It is perhaps the case that the establishment of a professional society for marine surveyors might be considered overdue.

Section One

Determining the Quantity Loaded or Discharged

Draft Surveys

Draft surveys are a convenient and economical means or ascertaining the quantity of cargo loaded in, or discharged from a ship. A well conducted survey is capable of achieving an absolute accuracy of $\pm\, 0.5\%$, which is as good, if not better than other systems of direct weighing which are available, and it is the only system with the advantage of consistency, i.e. the same yardstick is used for both loading and discharging.

General Remarks

Ideally, while the survey is in progress, the ship should be upright, with a trim of not more than one metre by the stern, lying in still water, with the ballast tanks either full, (pressed up) or empty. Any other conditions give rise to a host of corrections, which increase the probability of errors.

The co-operation of the ship's officers is essential during the survey, as ballast, bunkers, fresh water or stores, must not be moved, and all information and tables given to the surveyor must be accurate and up to date. The use of a work sheet and tank sounding sheet along the lines of that shown below is recommended.

Reading the Draft

The draft is read on both sides of the ship, at the forward, aft and midships positions. These are usually the only positions at which the draft is marked, though occasionally on large ships, draft marks are found on the shoulder and quarter. This should be standard practice, as it would give more accurate results, though some modification would be required in obtaining the mean draft with which to enter the tables.

Care must be exercised in obtaining the readings, which should be read from

DRAFT SURVEY — TANK SOUNDINGS

Ship ....

Survey Number .... Date ....

	Initial/Interim						Interim/Final					

Ford .... **Aft** .... **Ford** .... **Aft** ....
Port .... **Stbd** .... **Port** .... **Stbd** ....
Trim .... **List** .... **Trim** .... **List** ....

Tank	Obs. S'dg	Trim Corr	List Corr	Corr. S'dg	Vol.	Mass	Obs. S'dg	Trim Corr	List Corr	Corr. S'dg	Vol.	Mass
Total							**Total**					
Density		x					**Density**		x			
Mass							**Mass**					
Corr. for Density (1025-+)							**Corr. for Density (1025-+)**					
Corr. Mass							**Corr. Mass**					

Surveyor

a position as close to the waterline as practicable, so as to reduce the error of parallax to negligible proportions. Generally, it is preferable to read the offside drafts from a boat, as this provides a more stable platform than a ladder.

If the draft is read, while the ship is in an appreciable tideway, an error in reading the draft will be induced due;

    (a) to the apparent movement of the ship through the water, and

    (b) the build-up of water against the leading edge of a stationary object standing in moving water.

It is possible, provided the rate of flow of the current is known, to calculate the bodily sinkage, and the change of trim due to the apparent movement through the water. It is however, extremely difficult to obtain the amount of build up against the leading edge with any degree of accuracy. It is therefore prudent, to wait until the tide flow is negligible, before doing the survey.

If the sea conditions are such that waves make an accurate reading of the draft difficult to obtain, it may be advisable to use a draft tube. It must be used with caution, as errors in the reading will be induced if it is not set up vertically, and in certain circumstances the natural period of the system can give a false reading. It is probably preferable in these conditions, if an accurate clinometer, graduated in minutes of arc is available, (the average clinometer supplied to a ship is not nearly accurate enough for this purpose) to read the draft on the sheltered side only, and to calculate the draft on the weather side from the formula.

$$D_1 = D \pm \frac{B}{2} \tan \emptyset$$

where D_1 = draft required

        D = observed draft

        B = transverse distance between the draft marks at the water line.

        $\emptyset$ = angle of heel

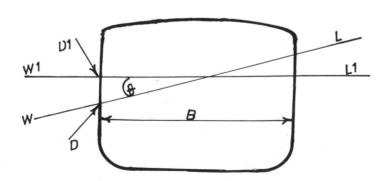

Differences in draft readings can occur at different times of the day or night. This is because of the differing expansion of the ship's deck being heated or

DRAFT SURVEY WORK SHEET

Date .... Initial/Interim/Final .... Time ....

Ship .... Survey Number ....

Cargo ....

Draft Ford port .... Cor .... Port	Port ....
Draft Ford stbd .... Cor .... Stbd	Berth ....
Draft Aft port .... Cor .... Port	....
Draft Aft stbd .... Cor .... Stbd	
Mean Ford Draft	D'weight ....
Mean Aft Draft	Gross ....
Trim .... Mean F and A Draft	Summer Draft.
Draft Midship pt ....,. Cor .... Port	....
Draft Midship sd..................... Cor .... Stbd	
Mean Midship Draft	Tonnages:
Mean F and A Draft	Requested ....
Mean of mean Draft	Survey ....;
Mean Midship Draft	Weightometer ....
Draft corrected for deformation	....
Displacement for	Weather Conditions. ....
.... x TPC/I	
Displacement from tables for draft	Draft Accuracy
Trim Correction	Estimate -/+ ....
....	....
List Correction	
Corrected Displacement	Density at berth
Density Correction (1025 -/+)	....
Displacement at observed density	Temperature
Deductions	....
Net Displacement ( )	
	LPP ....
Ballast	C of F ....
Fresh Water	Beam ....
Fuel Oil	ITM (1) ....
Diesel Oil	ITM (2) ....
Lube Oil	Difference ....
....	TPC/I (1) ....
Deductions	TPC/I (2) ....
	Difference ....
	....
Net Displacement	
Light Displacement (-)	Conversion Factor
Previously manifested cargo (-)	used Long/Metric
Stores and unknown Weights (constant)	....
Net Displacement ( )	(constant) average
Net Displacement ( )	figure previous voy's
Cargo loaded/discharged	....
(if part cargo) hatches	....

Surveyor ....

cooled in air and the ship's bottom being in water at virtually a constant temperature. The draft differences are usually small, though noticeable, but no allowance can be made for this phenomenon.

Some vessels are fitted with gauges to read the draft from a remote position. Generally drafts obtained by these means should not be used for surveys, as errors can and do creep in.

In good conditions, the normal degree of accuracy in reading the draft will be in the order of ± 2 cm, but in all surveys an assessment of the accuracy to which the draft has been read, and a description of the weather, should be given.

Correction to Draft Readings

The displacement scales of ships are based on the drafts of the various water lines parallel to the keel, and the drafts are presumed to have been taken on the fore and aft perpendiculars, in the case of the forward and after drafts, and LPP/2, in the case of the midship draft. Where the draft marks are not placed in these positions, a correction becomes necessary if the vessel is not on an even keel. Generally as the draft can only be read to an accuracy of ± 2 cm it is acceptable to round these corrections off to the nearest half centimeter.

These corrections are usually available in tabulated or graphic form but in ships where this is not so, the correction must be calculated. The distance between the draft marks and the appropriate perpendicular is obtained from the scale drawing of the ship.

$$\text{Correction} = \frac{\text{Distance between draft marks and perpendicular} \times \text{Trim}}{\text{LPP}}$$

where LPP is the distance between perpendiculars.

The application of the correction depends on the relationship of the particular draft mark in question to the perpendicular, but in most ships if ship trimmed by stern, minus to forward draft, plus to aft draft. If ship trimmed by head, plus forward draft minus to aft draft.

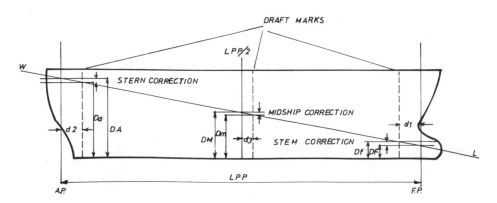

where

LPP	=	Distance between perpendiculars.
FP	=	Forward Perpendicular
AP	=	After perpendicular
Df	=	Draft at forward marks
DF	=	Draft at forward perpendicular
Da	=	Draft at aft marks
DA	=	Draft at aft perpendicular
Df $\sim$ Da	=	Apparent trim
Dm	=	Draft at midship marks
DM	=	Draft at LPP/2
d_1, d_2, d_3	=	Distance between draft marks and perpendiculars.

Stem Correction

Let the stem correction = x

then $x : d_1 = (Df \sim Da + x) : (LPP - d_2)$

thus $x = d_1 \dfrac{(Df \sim Da + x)}{LPP - d_2}$

which can be simplified without losing much accuracy into

$$x = d_1 \frac{(Df \sim Da)}{LPP}$$

Stern Correction

Let the stern correction = y

then $y : d_2 = (Df \sim Da + y) : (LPP - d_1)$

thus $y = d_2 \dfrac{(Df \sim Da + y)}{LPP - d_1}$

which can be simplified without losing much accuracy into

$$y = d_2 \frac{(Df \sim Da)}{LPP}$$

Midship Correction

Let the midship correction = z

then $z : d_3 = (Df \sim Da + z) : LPP - (d_1 + d_2)$

thus $z \doteq d_3 \dfrac{(Df \sim Da + z)}{LPP - (d_1 + d_2)}$

which can be simplified without losing much accuracy into

$$z = d_3 \frac{(Df \sim Da)}{LPP}$$

6

Measuring the Weight/Volume Characteristic of the Supporting Medium

It is important to obtain a representative sample of the water the vessel is floating in, so that a density can be accurately determined. It must be remembered that representative means not only typical physical composition, but also typical temperature. Samples should not be taken in way of scuppers or discharges, and the density must be recorded while the sample is still at its original temperature.

The sample of water should be obtained using a special sample bucket preferably fitted with a rose to restrict the ingress of water. If fitted with such a rose the sample bucket should be allowed to fall the full depth of the ship. If it is not fitted the sample should be taken at half the ship's draft. Samples should be taken near to the loadline. In some cases it may be necessary to take samples at the bow and stern as well in order to obtain a reliable average value, and it may be necessary to repeat the sampling procedures several times, in order to obtain a mean value of the density.

An hydrometer will only read correctly when immersed in a fluid at one specified temperature, it will be slightly in error at other temperatures owing to changes in own volume caused by expansion and contraction of the materials from which it is made. A table of corrections for this error should be supplied with the instrument, and the correction should always be applied, if the observed temperature differs considerably from the specified temperature, usually 60°F.

It is important to realise that the corrected reading of an hydrometer floating in water at say 80°F., will give the weight/volume relationship at 80°F., not what it would be if the water were reduced to 60°F.

The hydrometer used should be clean, and must not be damaged or dented, (in this regard it is preferable to use a glass hydrometer), and no air bubbles should adhere to the submerged portion. To avoid parallax errors the reading should be taken with the eye level with the bottom of the meniscus, while using a proper measuring vessel.

Determining the Known Weights

One of the more difficult jobs is to accurately determine the weight of ballast, fresh and boiler water, fuel, diesel and the lube oil and stores there are on board a ship. The surveyor should take or witness all the sounding of tanks necessary to determine these weights, both before and after the loading or discharge of cargo.

Except in the case of a deadweight survey, it is the difference between the various commodities at the light and loaded surveys that is important, and it is common practice to accept the Chief Engineer's figures for bunkers and to ignore the stores on board, taking any error involved in so doing into the 'constant'. Any error is the same in both the light and loaded survey and thus the final figure loaded or discharged is not affected. Any variance in these figures, between the two surveys, e.g. ship storing or bunkering, must be taken into account.

If the ship has even a small trim, the tank should not be recorded as full, but the surveyor should rather record the actual sounding. For even if the water is to the top of a 10 cm high sounding pipe, the tank is not necessarily full, when the ship is trimmed a metre or more by the stern. Pressing up a tank, when the ship is well trimmed by the stern will not necessarily fill the tank completely, as an air pocket could well be trapped. This pocket could be as much as 1% of the volume of the tank.

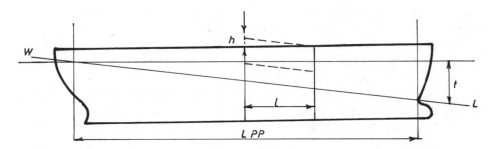

where

t = trim

l = length of tanks

LPP = length between perpendiculars

h = head of liquid required for a full tank

from similar triangles

$$\frac{h}{l} = \frac{t}{LPP}$$

$$\therefore h = \frac{tl}{LPP}$$

assume trim 1 metre by the stern, LPP 215 metres, length of tank 40 metres, depth of tank from deck level 18 metres, height of sounding pipe above deck 0.1 metres.

then h $= \dfrac{1 \times 40}{215}$

= 0.186 metres

therefore sounding for full tank is 18.186 metres, actual sounding is 18.1 metres, and the tank is not completely full.

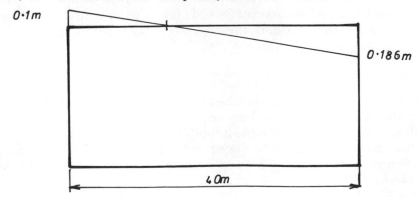

length of void space

40: $y = (0.1 + 0.186) : 0.186$

$\qquad y = 26$ metres

if the width of the tank at deck level is 6 metres, than the volume of the void space = ½ base × height × length

$\qquad = \frac{1}{2} \times 0.186 \times 26 \times 6$

$\qquad = 14.5$ cu. metres.

and if there are six such tanks, the error is in the order of 100 tonnes. Usually it is only the topside or combined topside double bottom tanks, which give this problem.

When ullaging ballast holds, care must be taken to identify and use the ullage port. If this is not in the centre of the hold, the ullage must be corrected for both trim and list, before entering the tables. Not all ships provide calibration tables for the ballast holds, and if this is the case, the ballast hold should be emptied before the survey is done. In some cases the calibration tables are only given to deck level, so that any water in the hatch coaming must be added to the total.

Some ships may have a ballast duct which it is not possible to sound. In this case in the light survey the tanks must be pressed up to ensure the duct is full. As there is no means of ascertaining that it is completely empty on the loaded survey, it should be assumed to be so, and a remark to this effect put in the survey report.

It is important that the weight/volume characteristic of any ballast is determined with the same degree of care, as used in determining that of the dock water in which the vessel is floating. It can be difficult to obtain samples of the liquid in some ballast tanks, but it should be done, as an appreciable change in the temperature of the ballast will alter its weight/volume relationship.

When entering the ballast tables, it is advisable to record the units in which the ballast is given, so as to prevent errors later. Special care is needed where the displacement is given in the imperial system and the ballast in the metric system, which is the case in some ships.

There are very few ships in which the ballast can be completely discharged, and it is usual to find a residual amount, which is usually more than most ship's officers expect. The actual amount remaining depends on numerous factors, among which are: the shape of the tank, the number of intercostals, the position of the suction pipe, whether or not there is a pad under the sounding pipe, and the vessel's trim.

It is important to remember that all soundings must be corrected for trim and list; and that a zero sounding does not necessarily mean no ballast remaining. Most ships will have some ballast remaining for a zero sounding.

If the ship has not got correction tables for trim, an approximate correction can be obtained from the formula,

$$\text{correction} = \frac{\text{Trim (cm)} \times \text{Tank length (m)}}{2 \times \text{LPP}}$$

where LPP is the length between perpendiculars.

NOTE: The correction so obtained is strictly only correct for rectangular tanks.

An approximate correction for list is much more difficult to obtain, so that if a ship does not have such tables, it should be brought upright, or with a list of no more than $\frac{1}{2}°$, before the soundings are taken.

The Constant

The 'Constant' is the difference between the displacement at any draft, and the known weights including the light displacement. It is usually calculated by the shipbuilder, but there is no standard format for the weights that are included. Thus this computation must be checked before a comparison is made between the 'constant' obtained at the survey and that calculated when the ship is built.

For our purposes the 'Constant' is badly named, for by the nature of its computation it must be a variable. The odds of having the quantity of lube oil and stores on board exactly the same at any two surveys are astronomical.

Other factors that affect the 'Constant' are mainly, the age of the ship (accretion of paintwork, rust, cargo residue etc.), mud in the ballast tanks, dunnage, lashing material, errors in reading the draft, errors in tank soundings, mispositioned draft marks, growth on the ship's bottom, one or both anchors on the bottom, incorrect bunker and oil figures, though others may be found from time to time.

Although the 'Constant' is variable, and is better known as 'Stores and Unknown Weights', it does serve as a guide to the accuracy of the survey, and a result within ± 100 tons of the mean figure, obtained over several surveys may be accepted. If the result obtained is outside these limits, the survey data should be checked, and if the same result is obtained, it may be accepted. In such cases, a remark to this effect should be made in the survey report.

Occasionally, a negative 'Constant' will be obtained, and as this is theoretically impossible, it is imperative the drafts, ballast and bunkers on board are double checked; bringing the ship to an even keel, if necessary. If, as sometimes happens, the result is still negative, then the error is usually in the draft marks or the light displacement. The 'Constant' thus checked, should be used, but a note to this effect is required in the survey report.

The 'Stores and Unknown Weights' can really only be obtained with the ship in the light condition, but computing a value with the ship in the loaded condition, using the manifested cargo figure, can given an indication of the likely out-turn. A variation from the average value, is the amount the out-turn is likely to differ from the manifested figure. If a negative value is obtained in this case, the error is almost certainly in the cargo.

The Weight/Volume Relationship

Definitions and Standards

The displacement of a ship is equal to the mass of the water displaced by the ship.

The mass of water displaced by the ship is equal to the underwater volume of the ship multiplied by the density of the water the ship is floating in.

The density of a liquid is its mass per unit volume, at a temperature t°.

The specific gravity of a liquid is the comparative density of that liquid at its actual temperature in relation to that of fresh water at 4°C.

The temperatures of water adopted as standard is usually one of the following:—

Metric System	4° Celsius	= 39.2° Farenheit
	15° Celsius	= 59.0° Farenheit
Imperial System	60° Farenheit	= 15.6° Celsius
	62° Farenheit	= 16.7° Celsius

and the more common standards are:—

Metric System 4°C, at which the density of fresh water is greatest, 1m³ weighs 1000 kg.

Imperial System 62°F, at which one imperial gallon of fresh water weighs 10lb., and has a specific gravity of 1.000

These differing standards, and the fact that the shipbuilders do not always state clearly what values they have used in determining the displacement, give rise to confusion.

Displacement Tables

Most shipbuilders provide only the saltwater displacement tables, without giving any information how these tables have been calculated. It is generally assumed that they have been made for seawater of density 1025 grams per centimetre³ at 15⁰C. (The density of seawater varies with temperature and salinity.)

In practice the tables are usually made by multiplying the calculated underwater volume of the ship at various drafts on an even keel, in freshwater of SG 1.000 and multiplying by 1.025. At 15°C, the specific gravity of fresh water is not 1.000, but is in fact 0.99913, (in other words 1m³ of fresh water at 4°C weighs 1,000 kg. but, at 15°C, 1m³ of fresh water weighs only 999.13 kg.). The underwater volume should therefore be multiplied by (1.025 × 0.999130) instead of 1.025.

This error makes a difference of about 100 tonnes in a displacement of 100,000 tonnes.

It would be preferable if ship builders were to give the freshwater displacement, SG 1.000 at 4°C, leaving the surveyor or ship's officers to calculate the corresponding salt water displacement.

Example:

(a) Fresh water displacement at 4°C for 10.00m draft even keel
65 970 m/tons

(b) Observed water temperature   20°C
(c) Observed Density   1 018 kg/m^3
(d) Specific gravity of fresh water at 20°C   0.99823
(e) Displacement corrected for SG of fresh water at 20°C
65 853 m/tons

(f) Salt water displacement for 10.00m even keel, density
1018 kg/m^3 at 20°C   67 038 m/tons

Provided the relevant information has been supplied by the shipbuilder, it would be possible to work back and use this method, but this should only be done, if it is used at both loading and discharging ports.

In practice, it is usual to enter the displacement tables provided, with the quarter mean draft, and correct this for trim, list and density to obtain the corrected displacement for the survey. It is assumed for this purpose that the tables have been calculated with the density at 1.025 grams/centimetre^3 15°C.

Sounding Tables

The sounding tables provided by the shipbuilder, for fresh and salt water tanks, usually show the quantity of water present

1) in cubic metres, or
2) in tons, for a particular sounding.

1) It is normal practice to obtain the tonnage by multiplying the volume obtained from the tables by the density, without making any allowances for temperature, the error in so doing being ignored.

2) With fresh water, the tonnage is obtained by dividing the volume by 36. Fresh water actually has a density of 35.92 pounds per cubic foot at 60°F, but the error in using the rounded off figure is usually small, and is ignored.

With salt water, the tonnage is obtained by dividing the volume by 35. It is then normal practice to apply a density correction to the tonnage obtained for any variance in density from 1.025 grams per centimetre^3 at 15^{0}C. It should be remembered however, that salt water strictly only has a density of one ton per 35 cubic feet at 60^{0}F, and at this density and temperature has a specific gravity of 1.026.

The sounding tables for oil tanks, usually show the quantity of oil in either gallons or cubic metres, for a particular sounding. In both cases the volume can be converted into weight, using the appropriate formula.

12

$$\frac{\text{Gallons at temperature} \times \text{Factor} \times \text{SG at } 60° \text{ F}}{224} = \text{Tons}$$

$$\frac{\text{Metres}^3 \text{ at temperature} \times \text{Factor} \times \text{SG at } 60°\text{F}}{1000} = \text{Tonnes}$$

Correction for Deformation (the Quarter Mean Draft)

A deformation or deflection correction is necessary when the vessel is bent longitudinally, resulting in a hog or sag condition, which can be observed as a difference between the mean of the corrected fore and aft drafts, and the corrected mean midship draft. The correction is based on the assumption that a ship will bend in a smooth parabolic curve; though this does not happen, it is a reasonable assumption in most cases. This is just as well as most ships are not usually supplied with information concerning the form of the deflection curve.

It is essential to remember that the load line convention does not permit this correction to be taken into account when loading a ship to her marks. The sag will reduce the cargo on board, and an hog increase the cargo on board of a ship loaded to her appropriate load line.

There are various ways of obtaining this correction, and by far the most commonly used are:

(a) The double mean of means, or quarter mean draft, calculated as follows:-

(1) Corrected Ford, draft
Corrected Aft, draft
Mean fore and aft draft

(2) Corrected mean midship draft
Mean fore and aft draft
Mean of mean drafts

(3) Corrected mean midship draft
Mean of mean draft
Quarter mean draft

which can be expressed as follows:—

$$\frac{DF + DA + 6DM}{8} \quad \text{or} \quad DM \pm \tfrac{1}{4}(DM - DFA)$$

the sign of the correction in the latter case being negative for sag, and positive for hog.

Where DF is the fore draft. DA is the draft, DM is the mean midship draft, DFA is the mean fore and aft draft.

(b) From the formula.

$$\Delta d = TPC - \frac{4 \times MTC}{LPP}$$

where Δd is the hog/sag correction in tonnes/centimetre

TPC is the tonnes/centimetre immersion for the mean draft in question
MTC is the moment to change trim one centimetre
LPP is the distance between perpendiculars
the correction is negative for sag, and positive for hog, and is applied to the displacement obtained for the mean midship draft.

Correction for Trim

The vessel's displacement scale is usually calculated for one given condition, which is almost invariably that of even keel. It follows therefore, that if the vessel is not in that condition, either:

(a) The displacement obtained by entering the tables with the quarter mean draft be corrected, or

(b) The draft must be corrected before entering the tables. It should be noted:

(1) That because a ship trims, not about its midpoint but about its centre of floatation, that for a given midship draft, the displacement will vary to some extent with trim.

(2) A change in the density of the water, will cause a ship to alter its trim.

It is frequently found that the trim correction tables supplied to ships, are based on the formula;

$$\text{Trim Correction} = \frac{\text{TPC} \times \text{Distance LCF from midships} \times \text{Trim}}{\text{LPP}}$$

Where TPC is Tons per centimetre immersion
LPP is Length between perpendiculars
LCF is the longitudinal centre of floatation.

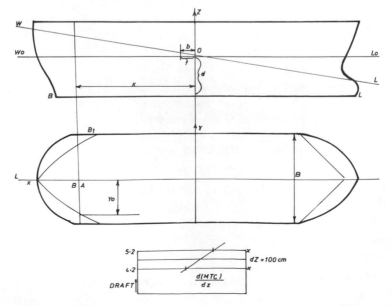

14

While the formula is basically correct, it does not go far enough, and an error is induced which can be considerable especially if the ship has a large trim. This error is removed by using Nemoto's formula.

$$2 \int_d^{d + x \tan \emptyset} y dZ = 2y x \tan \emptyset +$$

$$\frac{2(x\tan\emptyset)^2}{2!} \frac{(dy)}{(dZ)} + \frac{2(x\tan\emptyset)^3}{3!} \frac{(d^2y)}{(dZ^2)} + \dots$$

the difference of volume made by WL and W_0L_0 is obtained by integration over the ship's length, and becomes;

$$V = Ab \frac{(t)}{(L)} + \frac{1}{2}! \times \frac{dI}{dZ} \frac{(t)^2}{(L)} = \frac{1}{3}! \times \frac{d^2I^3}{dZ^2} \frac{(t)^3}{(L)} + \dots$$

if the third and subsequent terms of the equation are ignored as being negligible, the equation can be rewritten for the difference of displacement as follows;

$$d = TPC \times dC \times \frac{Trim \times 100}{LPP} + 50 \times \frac{dM}{dZ} \times \frac{Trim^2}{LPP} \quad or$$

$$d = TPI \times dC \times \frac{Trim \times 12}{LPP} + 6 \times \frac{dM}{dZ} \times \frac{Trim^2}{LPP}$$

where d is the trim correction for displacement
    TPC is tons per centimetre immersion
    TPI is tons per inch immersion
    dC is the distance of the centre of floatation from midships
    $\frac{dM}{dZ}$ is the change in trimming moment per metre (foot) of draft.

If the trim by the stern is regarded as positive, and by the head negative; and distance of the Centre of floatation aft of midships is positive, and forward negative, then the correction becomes
    Trim by stern (+), C of F abaft 0 (+), correction positive.
    Trim by stern (+), C of F ford 0 (-), correction negative.
    Trim by head (-), C of F abaft 0 (+), correction negative.
    Trim by head (-), C of F ford 0 (-), correction positive.

NOTE: An approximate $\frac{dM}{dZ}$ can be obtained from the formulae

$$\frac{dM}{dZ} = \frac{30(TPI_1^2 - TPI_2^2)}{B} \quad or \quad \frac{7.2(TPC_1^2 - TPC_2^2)}{B}$$

where TPC_1/I_1 is the TPC/I 50cm/6in. more than the mean draft.
    TPC_2/I_2 is the TPC/I 50cm/6in. less than the mean draft.
    B is the beam.

Approximate Correction for List

At the ends of the ship, where it is not wall sided in way of the waterline, the wedge emerging from the water is smaller than the wedge being immersed. To correct this difference, the ship lifts out of the water until the emerging volume is equal to the newly immersed volume. For a small ship, the correction will be small and could probably be neglected, provided the list is not more than say two degrees. However for a large ship the error in the calculated ship mass when this effect is ignored may be significant.

Few ships have tables giving this correction, and with data currently supplied to the ships, it is difficult to make an accurate correction, but the following formula will give an approximation. It would however, be better to have the ship upright for the survey.

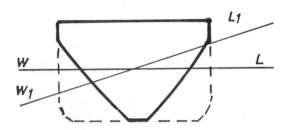

$$\text{Error} = 6(\text{TPC}_1 - \text{TPC}_2) \times (\text{Dm}_1 - \text{Dm}_2)$$

where DM_1 and DM_2 are the midship drafts on each side of the vessel.
TPC_1 and TPC_2 are the tonnes per centimetre corresponding to those drafts. The correction is always positive.

Correction for Density

In practical survey work, the assumption that the displacement tables and tank calibration tables, where the quantity of water is expressed in mass, have been made for seawater of density of 1025 grams/centimetre^3 at 15^{0}C, is accepted. Thus, if the observed density is at variance with this assumption, a correction becomes necessary to alter the mass to that corresponding to the observed density.

It must be remembered, that if the temperature of the water is markedly different from that for which the hydrometer is calculated, than the reading obtained must be corrected from the correction tables supplied with the instrument.

The correction to apply is obtained from the formula
$$\text{Correction} = \text{Displacement} \times \frac{(1025 - \text{observed density})}{1025}$$
the correction is positive if the observed density is greater than 1025, and negative if less than 1025.

Alternatively the corrected value can be obtained directly from the formula.
$$\text{Corrected Displacement} = \frac{\text{Displacement} \times \text{observed density}}{1025}$$

Deadweight Survey

Occasionally it is necessary to determine the mass of cargo on board a vessel, from the loaded survey only. In this case the basic procedures followed to obtain the displacement are exactly the same, but it becomes important to carefully check all non-cargo weights, as we are not dealing with a difference of displacements obtained from two surveys, where a lot of these are common to both and thus cancel out.

Procedures for obtaining the quantity of fresh and ballast water remain the same, but the surveyor must check all fuel tanks, and not rely on the Chief Engineer's figures.

The make up of the constant calculated by the shipbuilder must be examined, and allowance made for any known variance in the weights which go toward its makeup, or are not included therein. In addition, if the ship is old, then it may be advisable to make some allowance for an increase in the constant due to the age of the ship. A rough rule of thumb for this increase, is to add $\frac{1}{2}\%$ of the constant for each year of the ship's age.

All the known weights, including an allowance for stores and unknown weights (constant), are added to the ships light displacement, and the sum subtracted from the corrected displacement obtained for the ship's draft; the difference being the cargo on board.

A note must be made in the survey report of any 'variance' included in the 'constant'.

Ullage Surveys

General Remarks

Although it is possible to determine the amount of cargo loaded aboard or discharged from a tanker by draft survey, it is more usual to determine this quantity by ullaging the tanks, and thus finding the volume occupied by the product and knowing or ascertaining its density, calculating the tonnage. It is common practice for the quantity to be determined both in the ship and at the shore tanks, and it is usual to find a slight discrepancy between the two results. A suitable ullage survey work sheet is seen below.

Occasionally ullage surveys are used to determine the quantity of bulk cargo loaded aboard a ship, usually when it is loaded as a slurry, but this method is not as accurate as a draft survey.

Ullaging (Tankers)

Before and after completion of loading or discharging, every tank must be ullaged or inspected, even tanks that are said to be empty, as product can leak into them for a variety of different reasons. The ship's cargo to sea valves should also be checked and padlocked before discharge or loading commences.

At the time of ullaging the tanks, the draft must be read, and a note made of the trim and of any list. The ullage read must then be corrected for these factors, before entering the tables. The appropriate corrections for ullage are always tabulated.

The temperature of the product in each tank must be taken at the same time as the ullaging is done. It is normal to find some slight variation in temperature between the various tanks.

Sampling

It is important to ensure that all equipment used for sampling or for the storage of samples is scrupulously clean. The containers should be rinsed with the product from the tank in question before taking samples.

With most products, a running sample is sufficient to obtain a representative density. A running sample is obtained by allowing the sample can or bottle to fall freely through the fluid and then withdrawing it at a constant speed.

Where a product covers a wide range of densities and is prone to layerization in storage tanks, samples must be obtained from a minimum of three different levels in the tank and a composite sample made to determine the density in that tank.

ULLAGE SURVEY WORK SHEET

Date .... Time .... Berth ....

Ship .... Survey Number ....

Cargo ....

Tank Number	Ullage Observed	Correction List Trim	Corrected Ullage	Gross Capacity	V.C.F.	Net Capacity	Observed Temp.	Density	Quantity
Totals/Average									

Density at 60° Load Port .... Volume Correction Factor ....

Density at 60° Discharge Port ....API ....

Density at   Discharge Port ....

Draft Ford .... Aft .... Trim .... List ....

_____

_____

Cargo Quantity   **Metric/Long Tons.**

_____

Surveyor

A further composite sample is made from those composite samples from the individual tanks so as to obtain the density, for the quantity determination.

It is sometimes advantageous to compare the figure obtained from the total volume and the final composite density against the summation of the quantity determined from the individual tanks.

Density Determination

The determination is carried out in accordance with the Institute of Petroleum American Standard Test methods, and usually one of two is adopted. This should be witnessed by the surveyor.

1. *Using an Hydrometer*

    The sample is poured into a large glass beaker sufficiently wide enough so that there is sufficient space around the hydrometer to prevent capillary action. It is normal practice to record the temperature first, stirring or mixing the product while doing so. Before placing the hydrometer in the beaker, check that all bubbles that were trapped in the liquid have risen to the surface and dispersed. If bubbles remain in the liquid a false reading will be recorded.

    Allow the hydrometer to settle once it has been placed in the liquid and when it has reached equilibrium, read the density taking the reading from the bottom of the meniscus. If the liquid is opaque, the reading has to be made from the top of the meniscus, and a correction factor, which can be found in the OP/ATSM tables applied. The temperature of the liquid should be taken before and after taking the reading from the hydrometer, to ensure that this has not changed during the test.

    This gives us the density at the observed temperature, and it may be necessary to correct this reading for the expansion or contraction of the hydrometer, if the observed temperature is markedly different to that for which the instrument is calibrated. This corrected density must now be converted to the standard temperature being used, usually 60°F although 15°C and 20°C are sometimes used.

    $$Dts = Dto \times CF \times (ts - to)$$

    where D = density

    ts = standard temperature
    to = observed temperature
    CF = Conversion factor

2. *Capillary – Stoppered Pyknometer Method*

    The density in gm/ml at the observed temperature is calculated as follows:—

    $$Dt = \frac{(W_2 - W_1) + C}{Wt_1}$$

Where Dt = density at the observed temperature
 W_1 = weight of the empty Pyknometer
 W_2 = weight of pyknometer plus sample
 Wt_1 = water equivalent to pyknometer at observed temperature —
 density of water at observed temperature in gm/ml
 C = Air Buoyancy correction.
 Wt_1 and C are obtained from the tables
The density obtained must be converted to that at standard temperature.

Calculation

The tonnage in the tanks is calculated from the formula

$$\frac{Vto \times VCF \times dts}{1000} = \text{Metric tons (if volume in litres)}$$

$$\frac{Vto \times VCF \times dts}{224} = \text{Long Tons (if volume in gallons)}$$

where Vto = volume at observed temperature
 VCF = volume correction factor
 dts = density at standard temperature

The volume at the observed tank temperature, is obtained by entering the ship's calibration tables, using the ullage of the tank in question which has if necessary been corrected for trim and list. The volume correction factor is obtained from the IP/ATSM tables, Table B, the arguments being observed density and the temperature of the product.

If all tanks contain the same product, and the temperature difference between them is small, the volumes for the individual tanks can be added together, and the temperatures obtained and averaged, so as to reduce the computations necessary. If, however, there are different products in the tanks or the variation in temperature exceeds 5°, then the quantity in each tank must be calculated individually.

So as not to delay the ship, when doing a survey on discharge the figures should initially be calculated using the densities obtained at the loading port, and if the answer obtained is within 0.5% of the B/L figure the surveyor can allow discharge to commence. Cargo outturns within 0.5% are usually accepted commercially without question but obviously with the larger ships now in service this can be a sizeable amount, and it is felt the result should be well within this limit before being accepted.

If the difference is larger than 0.5% an investigation must be made into the discrepancy. Should, after the investigation which must include checking the ullages and temperatures obtained, the answer is still the same the surveyor should advise his principals to give the Master a Letter of Protest, informing the Master of his intention to do so.

In either case the figures obtained must be recalculated when the discharge densities have been obtained.

Shore Tanks

General Remarks

Prior to the arrival of the ship, and after completion of loading or discharge the shore tanks must be measured (dipped or ullaged, in conjunction with the installation personnel and/or customs.

Measurement

Unless there is a large amount of sediment in the bottom of the tank, a dip should be taken. As a check, when taking the dip, read the height, at the lip of the dip point when the bobbin of the measuring tape is just touching the bottom of the tank, and compare this with the overall tank height which should be inscribed on a plate near the dip point hatch.

If there is a large amount of sediment in the tank an ullage must be taken instead of the dip. In either case, a second measurement must be taken which should coincide with the first. If there is a discrepancy, the measurements must be taken until such time that two measurements coincide.

Some shore tanks have more than one dip point, and should this be the case, the average of the dips obtained from each point is used for calculation purposes.

If the roof of a floating roof tank is in the low or empty state never climb down onto the roof, as the area could be filled with highly volatile and poisonous gases.

When taking a dip in a heavy viscous liquid, the tape must be allowed to remain in the product for about ten seconds, so as to allow the indentation in the surface of the liquid, made by the tape entering the product to level out. With light products, the tape must be removed as soon as possible after the bobbin touches the bottom of the tank, as there is a tendency for the surface liquid to creep up the tape.

Water Dips

With petroleum products a check for water in the tank is always necessary.

For surface water the only practical way of determining its depth is to use a 'thief', this is a glass tube narrowing at each end, with a stopper at one end. Lower the thief into the product and allow time for the liquid to reach equilibrium. Once this has been reached, place the stopper over the top, and retrieve the thief. The water layer will remain on top of the product in the thief and can be measured.

For bottom water, a thin layer of water paste is smeared on the bobbin of the tape which is then lowered into the tank until it just touches the bottom. Allow the tape to remain there about twenty seconds and withdraw it. When taking dips of viscous or black products, it may be necessary to wash the bobbin with kerosene in order to see the water paste, and it is extremely doubtful if a clear cut straight line will be obtained. Normally only spots of colour change will be found, and the surveyor should assume that the highest spot represents the level of the water.

Obtaining the Temperature

If the tank is heated, the temperature should be read at different depths in the tank, the number depending on the quantity of product in the tank. Usually though, a maximum of three will suffice and the results averaged. If the tank is not heated then one temperature reading will usually suffice, but attention must be paid to the ambient temperatures, which can affect the temperature in the tank. For this reason the temperature should be taken, when ever possible from the centre of the tank.

If one is using a thermometer held in its own case it should be allowed to remain at the required depth for at least thirty seconds, before being withdrawn. The reading should be taken while the thermometer is still in the dip hatch, and taken as quickly as possible as the ambient temperature can have a marked effect. Similarly if using a loose thermometer, the sample bottle should not be taken out of the dip hatch, until the temperature has been read.

Shore Lines

The shore lines to the tank must always be checked,
    (a)   to ascertain if the line is full or empty and
    (b)   if full, that the product in the line is the same as that which the ship is to discharge or load.

To check if a line is full, bleed the line at the highest point along the line that it is posible to do so. If when the valve is cracked open product appears the line is assumed to be full. If no product appears the line is either only partially full or empty. In the latter case open the main valve to the tank on the line in question so as to pressurise the line, taking care not to include the flexible hoses, which are connected to the ship. If the main valve is not open when the tank is first measured, a check dip should be taken to ensure that nothing has drained from the tank to the line. The survey report must state the condition of the line before and after discharge or loading.

Table giving the approximate volume of a 3 metre length of pipe of various diameters.

Diameter	M³	Imp. Galls.
6"	0.05	12.07
8"	0.10	21.46
10"	0.15	33.53
12"	0.22	48.27
14"	0.30	65.71
16"	0.39	85.82
18"	0.49	108.62

Volume Correction Factors

Ethyl Alcohol	0.00083 per °C	Oil 1.076 - 0.9665	0.000347 per °F
50% Caustic Soda	0.00026 per °F	Oil 0.9659 - 0.8504	0.000395 per °F
Benzene	0.00066 per °F	Oil 0.8499 - 0.7758	0.000497 per °F
Toluene	0.00059 per °F	Oil 0.7753 - 0.7242	0.000607 per °F
Styrene	0.00054 per °F	Oil 0.7238 - 0.6725	0.000710 per °F
Orthoxylene	0.00053 per °F	Oil 0.6722 - 0.6420	0.000812 per °F
Metaxylene	0.00054 per °F	Oil 0.6417 - 0.6278	0.000852 per °F
Paraxylene	0.00055 per °F	Oil 0.6275 - 0.0611	0.000903 per °F
Coconut Oil	0.00035 per °F		

Ullage Survey Slurry Ore Carriers

Occasionally it is necessary to ascertain the quantity of ore loaded as a slurry aboard a bulk carrier in sea conditions which render it impossible to do a draft survey. The only answer is a ullage survey but it must be stressed that this is not as accurate as a draft survey.

The ullages should not be taken until the vessel has dewatered and should be taken in at least eight positions, spaced equidistant over the hold and the results averaged to obtain a figure, with which to enter the tables.

The quantity loaded is then found from the formula
$$T = V (SG + WE) \times (1 - VR)$$
where

T = quantity loaded
V = volume
SG = Specific Gravity of the dry ore
WE = Washing effect (1)
VR = Void Ratio (2)

(1) Washing effect is the slight increase in the bulk density due to the ore being wet. It may be ignored without an appreciable loss of accuracy.

(2) Void ratio is the ratio of the sand particles to the void space in a bulk sample.

Section Two

Determining the Condition of Hull and/or Equipment

Surveying Small Hulls

General Remarks

Usually a Marine Surveyor only surveys hulls that do not come under the jurisdiction of a Classification or Government Authority and ideally he should be well acquainted with small boat construction, and the type of boat he is required to survey. Surveys can of course be done without this specialised knowledge, but the surveyor is in a much more difficult position and must take great care that nothing of consequence is missed during the survey.

It is wrong to assume that unless a boat is falling to pieces that she is in good condition. All boats have some defects, and most have some inbuilt problems, either present or potential.

The only effective way to examine a boat is to take it apart, so that each section can be carefully examined but as this is impractical the surveyor should follow a middle course between doing unnecessary damage, to ascertain the condition of the scantlings and doing a superficial examination, that will not find hidden defects. Small, possibly insignificant details in themselves should not be overlooked, for it is often from these, a surveyor can deduce what has gone wrong, and what may yet fail.

Known defects should be pointed out to the surveyor by the Owner, and/or the skipper, but as he cannot rely on this being done, it is advantageous if the surveyor is aware of waterfront gossip for quite often a chance remark will provide a clue to some defect, or give pointers to some weak section, in a boat or class of boats.

The Certificate

This document can only relate to the survey done, i.e., hull condition, equipment or whatever. Sea worthiness should not be mentioned or implied for this is a combination of boat and crew, and the surveyor though he may have seen the crew has not examined them for their knowledge of seamanship, nor does he have the authority to do so and just as important, he has not necessarily checked on the stability of the boat.

It should be remembered that the survey certificate is only a statement of the condition of the boat at the time of the survey and, the longer it is since the survey was done, the less likely it is to represent the true condition of the boat. Wnat is true today, is not necessarily true tomorrow.

Preparing the Boat for Survey

There is a basic minimum of preparation, which must be carried out, before a survey is commenced for unless it is done the surveyor cannot examine the hull properly.

The preparation necessary for a boat in apparently good condition is
1. to have all loose gear taken off
2. all the centre floor boards removed
3. all portable panels removed.
4. the anchor cables ranged
5. the bilges clean and dry
6. to ensure adequate lighting is available in all compartments.
   If during the survey anything amiss is found or suspected, or, if it is an older boat or one in apparently poor condition then further preparative work will be required, in addition to that already mentioned and will include.
7. all floorboards and
8. all semi-portable panels removed
9. all floatation tanks lifted out
10. all permanent ballast removed
11. some nominated keel bolts removed.
12. all hatches discharged.

A full survey cannot be done with the vessel afloat, though once the surveyor has examined the exterior and interior of the hull the survey may be completed with the boat in the water.

The Survey

Before boarding a boat in a cradle, it is important to examine the chocks to see that the boat is secure and unlikely to tip over, due to the movement on the boat. Special care should be taken, if the boat has a glossy fibre glass hull, as chocks and wedges do not grip easily on this surface.

A good surveyor will quickly develop his own routine for inspecting a boat, and once developed this should be strictly adhered to, so that nothing is missed. As a start a general look at the hull often pays dividends and any indentations or abrupt changes to the fairness of the hull can be marked for closer examination. Some boats are of course designed with hard chines, and as these are abrupt changes of direction, they should always be carefully examined. Internal abrupt changes, such as those at the deck edge, bulkheads and floors should also be carefully examined. Scantlings should be examined for signs of movement, which initially will usually show up as paint cracks and/or traces of leaks. Edges, such as butts, scarphs, bolt holes and sea outlets, are also potential trouble spots in this regard. An aide memoire is the word FACES, derived from the initial letter of the words, fairness, abrupt changes, edges and scantlings.

If gouges are found on the bottom of the hull it suggests that the boat may have been aground, and the surveyor should look for further signs of trouble, such as cracked or broken frames, and beam knees, that this accident produces. If damage or repairs to the boat are found the surveyor should in addition to carefully examining this area, examine that diagonally opposite, as due to a wracking effect, it is quite likely that further damage will be found. It is worth noting, that the damage can be in both the vertical or horizontal plane.

Should the bilges show a well defined high water mark or if the paint in the bilge is overlaid with a film of mud, then there is a possibility that the boat leaks. Other tell tale signs that may be present are loose areas of paint, small areas of rust, the bilge pump showing signs of being well used, or the floorboards with a aura of sogginess about them. The actual cause of any leak may be difficult to find, especially if it is in the bilge area. Leaks from an hatch corner, or bolt will usually be indicated by runnels where the water has dripped through. Other places that always require careful examination are all sea cocks, the propellor shaft glands, and the transducer. Odd small leaks which are generally difficult to explain may be the first sign of woodworm and should be carefully examined.

When a vessel has internal ballast that is not being removed for the survey special attention should be paid to the area around the edge of the top layer. Any water which collects and lies in a hollow in this area could ultimately cause trouble.

Wooden Hulls

Wood can be tested by spiking or tapping, but it requires some experience to tell the difference between wood that is deteriorating and soft wood. So that it is advantageous for an inexperienced surveyor to spike various types of wood in known varying conditions to get the feel. The spike used should be of small diameter and very sharp, so as to damage the wood as little as possible. Sound wood will produce a ringing sound, when tapped, whereas water logged or rotten wood will give a dull sound. This difference is still there even when the wood is stiffened locally by a frame or bulkhead. Rotten wood also has a distinctive smell, which is easily recognisable, and it is this smell which is usually the first sign that rot is present.

Rot (both dry and wet) grows quickly, and if found should be cut out well beyond the signs of the rot. All the wood removed, and all shavings should be burnt immediately. Once the rot has been cut out, the whole area should be treated with a chemical, such as Cuprinol. All wood used to replace the rotten structure, should also be treated. The area should then be inspected every few months.

The ventilation of any compartment in which rot is found, should be closely examined, and if necessary modified, for rot thrives on moisture and lack of ventilation.

Deck seams, especially if open require examination, and it may be necessary to remove a small section of the caulking material for a closer look. Caulking is usually done with one of three materials:
(a) a white fluffy string which grows darker as it rots. It should not be soggy, hard or brittle or easily broken.
(b) Oakum or teased rope is brown and whiskery which as it rots loses its springiness and becomes brittle and
(c) Synthetic materials have a oily or greasy feel, which as they age, can slowly become water saturated.

The surface of any plywood present should be examined for signs of rumpling, which is an indication that delamination has occurred.

Wood can be damaged by electro chemical processes, caused by the action of two dissimilar metals, the wood first discolouring, then softening, and finally perishing so that it is important the hull be closely examined in the way of metal fittings.

Glass Fibre Hulls

On a sound glass fibre hull the whole surface is even without changes in the surface appearance. Some older white hulls turn yellow with age, while coloured hulls tend to fade or bleach. Yellowing along the wind and waterline will usually be caused by oily scum on the sea surface getting at and discolouring the fibre glass shell.

Blistering which is usually caused by osmosis, is a more serious problem, and all blisters found should be carefully examined. Bubbles, also can be a serious problem and require close examination. Generally if the bubbles are evenly spread, and are about 1.5 mm in diameter, and cover less than 5% of the hull surface, they may be accepted. If however they cover more than 5% of the surface or are larger than 1.5 mm in diameter, the hull will require to be tested. Bubbles which penetrate more than 1/5 the depth of the laminate or a collection of bubbles near a high stress location, such as a rudder gland, are serious and remedial action will be required.

Cracks in the gel coat can be a problem and are sometimes difficult to find, though kits are available to assist in detection. Scratches which penetrate the gel coat are as troublesome as cracks and remedial action will be required for both. The most usual cause of cracks is heat or excessive strain. If an area of dry chopped strand mat has been exposed, due to the gel coat being chipped away, immediate remedial action is required.

Fibre glass generally dislikes metal fastenings, so that the area around these, must be carefully examined, and should a keel bolt be removed from a

G.R.P. hull it is, as important to examine the area around the bolt hole, as it is to examine the bolt itself.

Other areas which require close examination, are those which are difficult to mould, such as a narrow skeg or hollow fin, as experience has shown that trouble is most likely to develop in these places. Careful note should be made of frames and stringers, which in well constructed boats, taper out, and not, as is sometimes found abruptly stopped.

If widespread defects are found or confirmation of quality and condition is required, a section should be cut out and tested.

Metal Hull

Steel hulls will usually deteriorate to a well established pattern, and it is normal to find the bottoms of compartments in a worse condition than the top, and floors more seriously corroded than the frames.

Areas which are difficult to get at tend to be neglected, and it is most important that the surveyor doesn't follow suit, but examines such places carefully. Seacocks and areas where dissimilar metals are in conjunction should also be carefully examined, as should the area around the propellor boss especially if the zinc anodes are very well worn, or have little or no wear.

If any section of plate is badly pitted, or if the surveyor has any doubts as to its thickness, he should have it drill tested, so as to get an accurate assessment of its thickness.

If the boat has any rivets, especially if it is an aluminium hull, they should be inspected, by tapping, as they have a tendency to become loose, partly through stress and partly corrosion. Welds should be examined as hair fine cracks are common particularly in aluminium boats.

On occasions, a light powdery substance will be found on the surface of unpainted aluminium plates, and although this aluminium oxide is a sign of corrosion, it is not serious as its formation tends to inhibit further corrosion.

Ferro Cement Hulls

Ferro cement, because of its high bulk density is usually only found in hulls over 10 metres in length.

The hull should be examined for many small pores and cracks, or a dusty surface, caused in the first instance by too wet a mix, and in the second by too dry a mix, both of which will allow water to get at the wire mesh causing rusting. Special care should be taken in underhung areas and on curves. External rust marks or areas where the mesh can be seen, should be noted and given closer examination for they usually indicate inadequate cover, or sometimes a faulty mix.

The hull should ring clear, and the hammer bounce elastically from a sound hull but where the render is too lean, or the adhesion poor, tapping with a light hammer will cause the mortar to flake or powder from the mesh. If the mesh is inadequate or damaged, the hammer may go through the hull.

Probably the most important aspect of surveying a cement hull is checking the thickness of the render. As a rough guide the cover over the mesh, should not exceed 3mm for though greater cover adds to the compression strength, it detracts from the flexural and tensile strengths which are important for a boat in a seaway. The surveyor should check the plans, or with the architect to ascertain the correct thickness, and should measure this, at any point he can, e.g., port holes, skin holes. In addition he should select, say 6 locations, and scrape back to the mesh a hole of 6mm wide x 50mm long, and measure the thickness of the render, resealing the hole with resin.

The cusps of mortar, especially around frames should be solid, and the edges of the cement, especially by way of skin fittings or the fastenings. If the deck and houses, are of different material, they should be protected against electrolysis and a check should be made that this is not taking place.

General

Although the hull forms a major part in any ship survey, there are other parts just as important, some of which unfortunately are occasionally neglected, with sometimes tragic results.

Steering Gear

The rudder should be examined, paying particular attention to the gudgeons and pintles, and the rudder alignment. Ideally the rudder should be put hard over each way during the examination. The steering gear itself should be examined paying particular attention to the cable or wire from the steering wheel. All boats with a remote steering position, should have an emergency tiller and the surveyor should see this fitted and tested.

Deck Fittings and Riggings

All deck fittings, such as bollards, fairleads, ventilator cowls, skylights, stanchions and railings should be checked, paying attention to the means, which should be adequate for the job, of securing these to the deck or bulkhead. Corrosion is likely in these areas in metal craft and should be watched for. Shackles, turnbuckles, ropes and wires, should be examined for wear, and if necessary replaced. In this regard, it is perhaps worth noting that stainless steel wire corrodes from the inside out, and becomes brittle with age, and does not have the visible tell-tale whiskers found with galvanised wire.

The winches should be run or worked, paying particular attention to any ratchet device and pawls. The mast step and lower section of the mast and any locking device if fitted, should be carefully examined for corrosion cracks or distortion, but unless the surveyor has any doubts, about the condition of the mast, it is not usually necessary to lower it for a close inspection of its entire length. Any hatch should be hose tested for watertightness.

Means of Propulsion, Tanks and Wiring

If the engine is the main means of propulsion, it and the associated auxiliaries should be surveyed by a qualified Marine Engineer. If the engine is only the auxiliary means of propulsion or the lighting plant it should at least be checked by a qualified mechanic. In both cases the necessary manuals recommended tools and spares should be on board. The electrical switchboard, and wiring should be checked by a qualified electrician or engineer.

The sails should be checked, paying particular attention to any chafing of the sail ropes, and the condition of the stitching. The sail should be examined for distortion, and the condition of the thimbles and bolt ropes noted. Any alterations to the sail usually shown by pleats in the sail or a row of empty stitch holes, should be noted.

Mildew, which will seriously effect cotton and canvass sails has little effect on synthetic fibres, but rust will affect all sail materials. Sails and ropes made from vegetable fibres can also rot. It is also worth noting that ropes made of synthetic fibre will lose strength with age, mainly due to ultra violet degradation, (the percentage loss being determined by the diameter of the rope). There is also some loss of strength due to prolonged exposure to sea water.

Lights and Shapes and Sound Signals

The boat must be fitted and equipped with the mandatory lights and shapes applicable to the class of vessel being surveyed. In addition the boats must carry the appropriate sound signals, usually a fog horn and bell. These must all be tested or sighted by the surveyor. All boats should also carry a radar reflector.

Kedge Anchor

In addition to the bower anchors, all boats should carry a kedge anchor as well. This anchor should have a short length of chain between the anchor and warp, which should be attached, so that it is readily available for use.

Life Saving Appliances

There must be sufficient life jackets on board for all persons that the boat is likely to carry, including if necessary smaller ones for children. All should be of an approved type, and checked that the fabric is sound.

In addition, there should be a safety harness, also complying with the appropriate standard, for each member of the working crew of a sailing yacht, and it is a good idea to have one or two on board a motor cruiser.

A lifebuoy with 30 metres of buoyant line, and a smoke/light signal attached, should be kept near the helmsman, and its condition and the brackets supporting the life buoy should be checked.

Any craft over 15 metres should carry an approved type of inflatable life raft, which should be serviced annually, and the surveyor should sight the relevant certificate.

Distress Flares and Signals

Any craft leaving the immediate port area should carry 2 red hand flares, and 2 orange smoke floats, and larger craft should carry 4 two-star red signals. If it is likely that the boat will operate off-shore, by which is meant more than seven miles off the coast, the two-star red signals should be replaced with red parachute rockets. The date of manufacture on all flares should be checked, and the flares should be in good condition, and should be replaced three years from the date of manufacture.

In addition all boats should have on board the small boat distress signal, for identification from the air.

Fire Fighting Equipment

Fire is the most frightening and possibly the most dangerous hazard faced at sea, and it is for this reason that most authorities recommend that motor yachts over 10 metres in length should be fitted with a fixed fire fighting installation, which if fitted must be checked regularly, and certainly during the survey.

All boats should have on board, a minimum of two fire extinguishers of an approved type, (2kg. dry powder extinguishers are probably the most suitable). Dry powder extinguishers will effectively extinguish an oil blaze which has reached a high temperature, but care must be taken, as the gases given off are liable to reignite, and cooling must be resorted to as soon as possible and if the boat is fitted with a powerful engine, an additional 4 kg dry powder should be supplied. The extinguishers should be checked every year, and the surveyor should see that this has been done.

A 9 litre bucket, with a lanyard attached, should be kept for fire fighting in an emergency which could if necessary also be used for bailing. In addition, a small axe, and a waterproof torch, with spare batteries should be kept in a locker near the helmsman.

Compass, Navigation Equipment

The compass should be checked, and if necessary swung for deviation. It is advisable to have a hand bearing compass on board, which can be used for steering in an emergency.

All yachts should be fitted with a clock and barometer and if it is intended to do longer voyages, a deck watch or chronometer, accurate enough for navigation purposes should be carried.

First Aid Kit

All boats should carry a first aid kit, and all outdated items should be thrown away and replaced.

Miscellaneous

All boats should have an emergency bag containing as a minimum, sailing twine, seizing wire, a selection of shackles and bulldog grips, a short length of canvas, palm and needle, a knife, marline spike, and a waterproof torch and spare batteries, which should be kept in a locker near the helmsman.

In a motor cruiser another bag should contain a full tool kit, engine manual, and for a petrol engine spare spark plugs.

All boats should be equipped with a boat hook.

Radio

All boats, in which is it intended to leave harbour limits should be equipped with a single side band radio, with at least 2182 kc/s fitted. This should be tested, by contacting the nearest coast station with it. The mandatory distress card should be displayed near the radio.

Distortion of the Hull

Occasionally distortion will be found in a boat, especially after grounding. or faulty building procedures and as a general rule, the maximum distortion, that should be allowed is in the order of,
(a) Variations in half beam — 15mm per metre of half breadth
(b) Twist in keel line — 9mm per metre of length
(c) Lack of plumb from centre line to keel — 9mm per metre of depth, at point of measurement.
(d) Lack of level at sheer — 15mm per metre of half breadth.

Rust and Steel Surface Preparation Grades

It is often advantageous to be able to clearly identify the degree of rust, and/or the degree of preparation required.

The following grades have been approved by the Australian Standards Association, and are taken from Swedish Standard SIS055900 — 1967.

Rust Grade

A. Steel surface covered completely with adherent mill scale, and with little or no rust.
B. Steel surface which has begun to rust, and from which the mill scale has begun to flake.
C. Steel surface on which the mill scale has rusted away, or from which it can be scraped, but with little pitting visible to the naked eye.
D. Steel surface on which the mill scale has rusted away and on which considerable pitting is visible to the naked eye.

Preparation Grades (Scraping and Wire Brushing)

It is assumed that prior to treatment, the steel surface has been cleaned of dirt and grease, and that heavier layers of rust have been removed by scaling.

St. 2.   Thorough scraping and wire brushing — machine brushing — grinding etc. The treatment shall remove loose mill scale, rust and foreign matter. Finally, the surface is cleaned with a vacuum cleaner, clean dry compressed air, or a clean brush. It should have a faint metallic sheen.

St. 3.   Very thorough scraping and wire brushing — machine brushing — grinding etc. Surface preparation as for St. 2, but much more thorough. After removal of dust, the surface shall have a pronounced metallic sheen.

Preparation Grades (Blast cleaning with various abrasives)

It is assumed that prior to treatment, the steel surface has been cleaned of dirt and grease, and that heavier layers of rust have been removed by chipping.

Sa. 1.   Light blast cleaning. Loose mill scale, rust and foreign matter shall be removed.

Sa. 2.   Thorough blast cleaning. Almost all mill scale, rust and foreign matter shall be removed. Finally the surface is cleaned with a vacuum cleaner, clean dry compressed air, or a clean brush. It shall then be greyish in colour.

Sa. 2.$\frac{1}{2}$ Very thorough blast cleaning. Mill scale, rust and foreign matter shall be removed to the extent that the only traces remaining are slight stains in the form of spots or strips. Finally the surface is cleaned with a vacuum cleaner, clean dry compressed air, or a clean brush. It shall have a uniform metallic colour.

Sa. 3.   Blast clean to pure metal. Mill scale, rust and foreign matter shall be completely removed. Finally the surface is cleaned with a vacuum cleaner, clean dry compressed air, or a clean brush. It shall then have a uniform metallic colour.

Once a steel surface has been prepared, it is referred to by its initial rust grade, and the degree of preparation that has been applied.
      eg. C Sa 2.

On and Off Hire Surveys

These are probably the most time consuming surveys of all, especially if the ship is a few years old, for every defect must be noted, and what is probably even more important, identified in such a way that someone else can find it, so that any new damage which has occurred during the period of hire can be found, and if necessary fixed.

The surveys must be done in daylight, with the hatches fully open and they should be empty and clean. There are no circumstances which can justify the survey being done at night or under artificial light, for in these conditions defects will certainly be missed.

It is usual to find two surveyors doing this survey, one representing the charterers, and the other the Owner, though it is not uncommon for the Owner to nominate the Master as his representative, in which case the surveyor will almost certainly be on his own.

The survey covers that area of the ship, in which damage can occur during loading or discharge, that is the deck, deck houses, cargo gear, hatch covers and holds, and usually includes in addition the determination of the bunkers on board, at a fixed time when the charter commences or finishes.

In order to miss nothing, it is best to follow a set pattern which is rarely varied, and the following pattern is recommended in carrying out the survey and in recording the damage in the survey certificate.
(a) Port side bulwark/rails and deck
(b) Starboard side bulwark/rails and deck
(c) Deck houses, and cargo gear
(d) hatch coamings and hatches
(e) Holds — port side, (saddle tanks, ships side, hopper tanks) forward bulkhead, starboard side, (saddle tanks, ships side, hopper tanks), after bulkhead, tank top.
(f) Bunker survey

Positive positioning is provided by numbering stanchions, rails, frames beams etc., always from forward to aft, top to bottom, and port to starboard. All the damage found must be noted. Where there are numerous dents in the tank top, it is common practice not to try and position all the dents, but rather to record, 'tank top indented overall'. If the indentations are deeper than about 6mm, the position should be recorded.

When doing the bunker survey, the tanks must be sounded in conjunction with the ship's Chief Engineer, and the specific gravity, which must be corrected for temperature taken from the bunker certificate, issued at the port of loading.

In addition the ship's particulars, and the dates of the following certificates, should be recorded in the survey:
(1) Certificate of Registry
(2) Safety radio certificate
(3) Safety equipment certificate
(4) Safety construction certificate
(5) Loadline certificate
(6) Deratting exemption certificate
as well as the time the on/off hire, took place, and the ships position at that time. If the survey took place at a different time and place to that of the on/off hire, then the time and place of the survey must also be recorded.

Less Common Surveys

Accident or Collision Surveys

On occasions where the responsibility for an accident is in dispute, a Marine Surveyor could be asked to investigate, and record all the relevant facts. All facts must be impartially recorded with no conclusions drawn or anyone judged (this is for others to do). As if this is done the report could be prejudiced.

Lay-up Surveys

Where a ship is to be laid up, it is imperative to check that the Underwriters' requirements have been carried out. If the lay-up is to be for any length of time, periodic inspections, will be required to check that the conditions on the ship have not altered.

Hydro-Static Survey of In-Service Heavy Duty Synthetic Rubber Hose

The pressures and percentage elongation stated, are in accordance with the Australian Standard for discharge hoses, at shore terminals. There are however different standards, for example, the OCIMF standard for an hose at a SBM, requires a test pressure, of 15 bar (225 psi), but the procedures laid down however are basically the same. A pressure recorder, of sufficient scope to cover the test pressures, will be required.

The procedures is as follows:—
(a) Lay the hoses out as straight as possible, and support on dollies, in order to allow free movement during the complete period of the test.
(b) Fill hose with water, venting all air, and apply a pressure of 0.7 bar (10 psi)
(c) Measure the overall length, (flange to flange), of each hose in the assembly.
(d) Increase pressure over a period of 5 minutes, to 5.25 bar (75 psi). Hold this pressure for 10 minutes, then reduce the pressure over a period of 5 minutes to zero.
(e) Raise the pressure over a period of 5 minutes to 5.25 bar (75 psi). Hold this pressure for 10 minutes.
(f) With the hoses at full test pressure, measure the overall length (flange to

flange) of each hose in the assembly.

(g) Inspect the hose for leaks local distortion, or any indication of weakness in the hose structure.

(h) Reduce the pressure over a period of 5 minutes to zero.

(i) After an interval of at least 15 minutes, raise the pressure again to 0.7 bar (15 psi)

(j) Measure the overall length (flange to flange) of each hose in the assembly.

(k) Release pressure on completion of test.

The elongation is given from the formulae

$$\text{Temporary working pressure elongation} = \frac{Lw - Lo}{Lo} \times 100\%$$

$$\text{Permanent elongation} = \frac{Lp - Lo}{Lo} \times 100\%$$

Where
Lw = the length of the hose at test pressure
Lo = the original length of the hose at 0.7 bar
Lp = the final length of the hose at 0.7 bar

For a new hose the temporary elongation shall not exceed 6%. For a used hose the temporary elongation shall not exceed 150% of the original elongation i.e. 9%. Permanent elongation should not exceed 2%. If any hose shows elongation in excess of these percentages, it should be replaced.

Section Three

Determining the Degree and Cause of Damage

Damage Surveys

The purpose of such surveys is (1) to assess fairly and dispassionately the degree of damage, and if possible to determine the cause of such loss or damage, and (2) to make recommendations to minimise, or make good the damage; though repairs, especially to the hull and equipment will normally come under the jurisdiction of Classification or Government Surveyors.

The Independent Marine Surveyor, will usually be attending such surveys for insurance purposes. and it is important that he has a working knowledge of the various Marine Acts, and the York-Antwerp rules.

It is the Surveyor's task to report on the cause, and the degree of loss or damage, and to assist, as far as is possible:
  (1) to prevent further loss or damage, and
  (2) to minimise, as far as possible, what loss or damage has already taken place.

He should therefore be careful of expressing or implying an opinion, on the question of the underwriter's or other person's liability, or of accepting responsibility, either himself, or on behalf of his principals for any damage, or for goods a consignee may wish to abandon.

The Surveyor should never recommend disposal of cargo, other than its delivery to the consignee, unless it is quite obvious, that such disposal would be beneficial to all parties, and even then, the consignee and the underwriter should be consulted. Equally, he should never agree to the reconditioning of damaged goods by the carrier. The consignee should see the goods in their damaged state, and if reconditioning is to be done, it should be done by the consignee, or a contractor approved by him. This may be more expensive, but it is more likely to satisfy the consignee, and thus avoid more serious consequences, though it does not mean that the cost of the repairs should not be checked.

Damage to Cargo

Notice

Notice of any loss or damage should be given to the carrier or carriers of the goods as soon as possible after it is first found, and the surveyor should advise his principal to give this notice: and also to invite the carriers and other interested parties to attend the survey, if this has not already been done.

The Survey

A joint survey, with the representatives of all parties concerned present, is the ideal survey, as if all agree on the measures to minimise any loss or damage; and later the degree of loss or damage, there is only left the question of liability, which does not form part of any survey. If agreement is not reached, than the joint survey will tend to allay any suspicion one party may have of the other: partial agreement may be reached, or at least the facts agreed on. For, if the sum involved is substantial, the matter may well have to be settled in court.

It is advantageous if the surveyor is frank and open in his dealings with others, as this not only promotes trust, but also may assist in finding out what the other party knows or may do. This does not mean, a Surveyor should automatically tell other parties all he knows or suspects; indeed there are occasions when this would be most unwise. Unfortunately, there are no hard and fast rules on this, and each case must be treated on its merits.

The names and positions of all those present at the survey should be noted and it can be of enormous help on future occasions, if for his own information, the Surveyor should note the attitudes and any other pertinant information of those involved.

Before the survey, the damaged goods should be separated from the sound goods, so as to make the survey easier and to prevent possible contamination of the sound goods from those which are damaged. This separation should be done by the consignee, who is the one who alleges that he has suffered a loss, but generally the cost of separating the goods will be borne by the underwriter.

Describing the Damage

It is important to give an accurate description of the damage, and if it can be ascertained, the cause of the damage. The latter is particularly important, for should the surveyor incorrectly determine, or describe the damage, the loss could well be borne by someone not liable for it.

Sometimes, it is extremely difficult to determine the cause of the loss or damage, and in such cases the Surveyor should be careful not to make statements that cannot be substantiated. It is also important, that the Surveyor certifies only what he has seen, which does not mean a complete examination is required in all cases. On occasions, after careful consideration of the facts, the Surveyor may be certain, that by the nature of the damage, an examination of part of the shipment will give a reasonable assessment of the whole, thus reducing the cost of the survey. In which case, a statement to this effect, and the reasons for it, must be put in the report.

In all reports, a description of the packing, (dimensions, type and condition of the materials used, mesh size, and lining if any) is required as this could help the underwriters in assessing if the packing was adequate, or met specification.

General terms should not be used to describe damage, as this may be quite misleading, and could lead to the liability being taken by the wrong party. For example 'Goods damaged by water'. Although this may well be the case, the description is far from complete, and numerous questions still have to be answered, such as;

(a) Is the water causing the damage fresh or salt water?
(b) If fresh water, is it from a leaking service pipe, rain during loading or discharge, or prior to or after these events? Or is it condensation in the hatch or case, or through being stowed adjacent to cargo with a high moisture content? Was the hold ventilation adequate, and just as important, was it properly carried out?
(c) If salt water, is it from a leaking filling or sounding pipe, corroded plates, a leaking tank, a leaking hatch cover, heavy weather, or collision or stranding?
(d) What percentage of the goods have been damaged?
(e) Of those damaged, what is the percentage depreciation of the goods?
(f) Can the damaged article be treated, or any damaged part replaced, so as to restore the article to its original condition? As a general rule, no restoration work should take place unless authorised by the underwriter.

Test for Salt Water

The Silver Nitrite test can be used to determine whether the damage is caused by salt water. The test consists of adding a few drops of the test solution to water in which the damaged goods, or samples of the damaged goods or packing, have been soaked.

When using the test, it must be remembered that some goods contain as a normal constituent, a certain amount of soluble chloride and that therefore sound portions of the goods should be tested as well. If the reaction is positive, it is a reasonable assumption that the positive reaction was caused by an outside source.

The test alone is not conclusive evidence of seawater, and the surveyor should look for and check other evidence. Where other evidence is not available, or doubt exists, or if, the damage is likely to be of a serious nature, a full analysis by a chemist should be made. The chemist should be provided with generous samples of both the damaged and sound goods, so that tests can be made on both and a comparison made.

The solution is made of;
    2 parts Silver Nitrite
    2 parts Nitric Acid
    2 parts Distilled Water
Nitric Acid is necessary in the solution, as some goods which contain alkalis will give a positive reaction to a solution of Silver Nitrite only. If the solution is prepared in advance, it must be kept in a dark bottle, as it deteriorates when exposed to light.

Ideally the water in which the goods or samples are soaked should be distilled water, but tap water can be used, provided it is first tested, to ensure it is free from chlorine. This is done, by placing about 10 cc. in a test tube, and adding about 5 drops of the test solution. If the water remains clear, it is free from chlorine; if not, it will turn milky, in direct proportion to its chlorine content.

The damaged goods, samples or packing, should be placed in a bowl and covered with warm distilled or tested water, and allowed to soak for five to ten minutes, which will allow time for any salt to dissolve. About 10 cc. is then placed in a test tube and about 5 drops of the test solution added. If salt is present, the solution will turn milky, and if the concentration is very strong, it will assume a curdled appearance.

Damage due to Two Causes

This is a problem that is sometimes faced, and if at all possible, the damage from each should be expressed as a percentage of the whole damage. In doing this, it should be borne in mind that the damage from one cause may not have prevented restoring the goods to their original condition, while the damage from the second cause could have made this impossible.

Degree of Loss or Damage

This is usually expressed as a percentage of the undamaged or sound value. The undamaged or sound value is usually taken to be the market value of the goods at their destination, or at the place of survey. If this is not known, an estimate of the value, can be made by adding to the invoiced cost of the goods charges such as freight, customs duty, landing and any prepaid charges. The damaged value is the market value of the goods in that state, which can be ascertained, either by sale of the goods, or by agreement with the assured and other interested parties.

It is advisable if at all possible to obtain agreement with the consignee and other interested parties, of the sound and damaged values, but the Surveyor must take care, either verbally or in his report to agree or imply, the monetary amount the insured is likely to recover.

Shortage in Weight/Packing

In cases of shortages in weight, weight notes should not necessarily be accepted as accurate and they should be checked as far as is possible. It should be borne in mind that some commodities, can due to natural causes, such as moisture content, lose or gain weight during a voyage. So that when faced with an apparent loss of weight, in addition to checking the invoiced weight, a reasonable number of packages, provided they are of apparent uniform weight and size, should be weighed, so as to obtain the average weight of each package.

Where articles are said to be missing from a package, a check should be made that there was in fact space in that package for the missing article. As packing slips are not always correct, other packages in the same consignment should be checked for the missing article. And checks should also be made with the agents, that the missing goods have not been shortlanded or overcarried to another port.

When a serious loss has occured, the actual case containing the goods should be kept for possible future examination.

Damage due to Contact with Other Goods

A check should be made where the damage occured, (before loading, in stowage, during the voyage or after discharge). The mate's receipts, the bill of lading, the stowage plan, shed records and carriers receipts should be examined for some indication could be obtained from these documents. If possible, the contaminant, or if it is infestation, the insect, should also be identified.

Pilferage

Where goods have been pilfered, in addition to quantifying the loss, it is important to try to establish how and where the loss occured.

This will mean examining the receipts given at the time of any transfer of the goods, the bill of lading and any other document which may help to establish when the pilferage occured. Even if the time and place of the pilferage occuring cannot be established with any degree of certainty, all details and preferably copies of these documents should be included in the report, together with recommendations, if any, on how the loss can be avoided or reduced in any future shipment. Details of any precautions taken by the carrier to prevent pilferage, must also be established, and included in the report.

Unidentifiable Goods

Problems are sometimes encountered, when either the goods did not initially have a distinguishing mark, or have lost their identification mark during transit. Where this has happened, and the goods are consigned to more than one consignee, care must be taken to avoid if possible allocating all the loss to one consignee.

Occasionally the shipment will have been damaged to the extent, that it is

42

impossible to determine the number of packages being delivered. When this occurs the bill of lading must be examined, comparing the figures on this document against the invoiced quantity. A check must also be made on any shortlanded or overcarried cargo.

Sampling

Where it is necessary to take samples for analysis, the Surveyor should take care to ensure that the sample obtained is fairly representative of the degree of damage, and it may also be advisable to take samples of the undamaged goods for comparison.

With bulk commodities, the individual samples should be mixed together and then coned and quartered, until the requisite size sample is reached.

All samples should be divided into three identical lots, packed, sealed and labelled, preferably in the presence of the consignee. One lot should be given to the consignee, the second sent for analysis by the surveyor, and the third retained as a reference sample in case a dispute arises at a later date.

Perils of the Sea

This is among the more important risks covered by Marine Insurance, and is one that will often cause the most headaches. This is due to the fact, that often too wide an interpretation is given to the clause, so that it covers all accidents that may happen at sea. Whereas the Marine Insurance Act gives it a more narrow definition;
        'fortuitous accidents or casualties of the sea'
ie. some chance accident must be involved, other than the ordinary action of wind and waves.

The Form of the Report

Comment has been made elsewhere on the Surveyor's report, but as it is essential to omit nothing of relevance to the survey, the following points are given as a guide.

(1) The details of the person or persons requesting the survey. (If they are agents, the name of the principals as well.)
(2) The date/s and location/s of the survey/s
(3) The names and designations of all persons present at the survey/s.
(4) Details of the carrying vessel/s. Port of loading and discharge, date of departure from loading port, arrival at discharge port, and list of intermediate ports with dates of arrival and departure.
(5) Description of the shipment, including place of origin and description of the damage.
(6) Facts regarding stowage.
(7) Details of loading and discharge.
(8) Details of transit, prior to loading and after discharge.
(9) The names and addresses of the shipper and consignee.
(10) Appropriate extracts from the ship's log book, and copies of any

protests made, if these can be obtained; if this is not possible, note the reason.

(11) Details of all documents examined, with particular reference to any remarks made in these, as to the condition of the goods.

(12) The dates on which the goods were tended and accepted for delivery, and the dates that the goods passed through the various stages.

(13) Details of the survey conducted, with a full description of the damage or shortage of details of the packing. If pilferage suspected, details of any action taken to reduce this loss.

(14) Facts regarding any damage or loss of weight, normally found on similar goods, at the port of discharge; and details of any customary allowances made in the trade.

(15) Description and comments on any analysis done, and if by an outside expert, his name, position and address.

(16) Details of any invoices inspected, duties and taxes applicable to the goods, including any rebate of customs duty applicable, due to the damaged nature of the goods.

(17) A list of all expenditure stated to have been made by the consignee or assured, and which he intends to make part of the claim, with comments if necessary.

(18) Details of any action taken to reduce damage and/or liability.

(19) Method used to ascertain the value of the goods in their damaged state.

(20) Details of applicable rates of exchange on date of sale or agreement.

(21) Details of any liability of third parties, and details of any claims made.

(22) A list of all documents attached and forming a part of the report, and a list of all references consulted.

Damage to Hull and Equipment

When doing a damage survey for hull and/or equipment, it is important to discover the root cause of the trouble, and not to accept the apparent reason until further investigation has shown beyond doubt that it is the real reason for the damage, and not the secondary one. For example, the topping wire of a crane may have parted, causing damage to both the crane and the lift. The apparent cause of the damage is the broken topping wire, but closer examination, may reveal that the weight of the article being lifted was beyond the capacity of the crane to handle. Although, this is the real reason for the damage, it is necessary to check that the crane is in current survey, and that the certificates for the various wires and shackles in the system are valid, and to obtain copies to accompany the report, and of course, a copy of any relevant log entry.

Pictures speak louder than words, and sufficient photographs, should be taken to illustrate the damage. Statements should be taken from any eye witnesses and the Duty and Chief Officers, even if they did not witness the incident. Occasionally, such interviews will reveal non-compliance with an order, or safety instruction. The Surveyor should be careful however, for it is not his job to accuse or judge anyone of wrong doing, he is there purely to ascertain and report the facts.

Not only should the immediate area be closely examined, so that the damage can be described, but also so should the surrounding areas, especially where damage to the hull is concerned, as related damage due to wracking effect or other causes might have occured. It is important to check that the damage, is consistent with the stated cause, as failure to do this could cause considerable embarrassment at a later stage.

The damage must be accurately positioned and described. Any technical terms used in the report, must be understood, not only by the surveyor but also by the parties for whom the report is intended.

Repairs

It is as well to remember, that when carrying out repairs, it is usually advisable to ensure that the existing structure is disturbed as little as possible, and that depending on the cause of the damage, the repairs are stronger than the existing structure.

Should a Surveyor be asked to supervise a repair job, it is important, that he check all stages of the repair to ensure that the specifications, are met. Outside experts should be called in for advice, if necessary.

Section Four

Determining the Suitability of a Compartment for Cargo

Cleanliness Surveys

When doing a survey for cleanliness, it is imperative that the surveyor knows as much as possible about the physical composition of the commodity to be loaded into a hold, tank or compartment, for this will obviously effect the degree of cleanliness that is required. Cargoes such as grain or premium zircon require the highest degree of cleanliness, while with others, such as coal, bauxite or iron-ore, the hatch only requires to be swept clean, although on occasions the charter party will require a higher standard of cleanliness, and then this becomes the governor factor.

Hatch Cleanliness Surveys:

Hatch cleanliness surveys should be done in daylight with the hatch covers fully open, so as to give the best possible light for the survey. If it becomes necessary to do a cleanliness survey at night, the surveyor should check that all parties interested in the survey are agreeable, and that the degree of hatch cleanliness is not a critical factor in loading. Further the lighting in the hold must be adequate, and arranged so as to minimise the casting of shadows. A wandering lead should be available to give additional light in areas requiring closer examination. The fact the survey was done at night, and the reason why should be stated in the report. It is important when doing the survey that the surveyor climbs down into each hold, for defects cannot be seen standing on the deck looking down into the hatch.

Although the degree of cleanliness is dependent on the type of cargo, the basic points to be looked for during the survey are the same. The tank top, bulkheads and sides of the hatch must be clear of residual cargo, mud, loose rust (the degree of rust allowable is very much dependent on the cargo to be loaded), or oil/grease, and for most cargoes the hatch must be completely dry before loading is allowed to start. With grain cargoes, the degree of infestation of the hatches can be critical, for depending on the degree and type of infestation, it may be necessary to fumigate the hatches, and although the responsibility for checking the infestation is usually the responsibility of a Department of Agriculture surveyor, it is in the interest of his principals that a Marine Surveyor co-operates fully, and points out any insects he finds to his colleagues.

The tank surfaces, and areas around any pipes, and the pipes themselves should be checked for tell tale signs of cracks or leaks, such as areas of loose paint, or small areas of rust, weeps, wetness, or a thin layer of mud in an area where one would not expect to find these things. The bilge suctions should be inspected, and must be clear and free. With some cargoes, it may also be necessary to check that the bilge suctions are working. After completion of the inspection the bilges/hat boxes should be covered with burlap or similar material. If the hold is also a ballast hold, the surveyor should check that both the suction and inlet pipes are blanked off.

It is usually easy to clean the tanktop, unless it has a permanent wooden ceiling in which case oil stains can be a problem. In areas difficult to get at, such as, ledges on the top of the hopper tanks, behind the protection plates of pipes, brackets and ledges in the top half of the hatch, at the bend of the hatch coaming or around manhole covers, a considerable build up of residual cargo can often be found, and a wise surveyor checks these and other places difficult to reach.

As the hatches are open when the holds are inspected, the hatch lids are often missed by surveyors and those cleaning the hatches, and a considerable quantity of residual cargo can often be found in the beams under the lids. If there is any rust in the hold, there will almost certainly be some under the hatch lids. It is usually difficult to inspect the lids, especially those that roll up, or have more than one leaf, so if a surveyor is in any doubt whether the hatch lids require cleaning or not, he should have the hatch closed. On re-opening the hatches it will be readily seen if the hatch lids require cleaning, for if they do, residual cargo and/or rust will have been shaken off, and fallen on to the tank top.

In addition, for grain cargoes the hatch must be free of odour, and all wooden gratings or boards in the hatch, must be completely dry. Green timber is not permitted. The cargo compartment must be structurally sound, cement boxes over holes or cracks are not permitted. Bulkheads and water-tight manholes should be checked for watertightness, and if the surveyor has any doubts about the watertightness of these, the tanks should be pressed up to test it. The weather deck hatch covers must be inspected, and if necessary hose tested.

Any bulkhead adjacent to a hold, in which grain will be stowed, which reaches a temperature in excess of 43°C, must be sheathed, as, must the bulkhead of a tank in which liquid is carried. All electrical wiring in a grain compartment must be disconnected or defused, and it is important that portable lights are removed when not in use.

Should the hatch fail to reach the requisite standard of cleanliness, the surveyor must advise the Master what work is necessary to bring the hold up to the required standard. He should also visit the ship at regular intervals while this work is being carried out, thus ensuring that as little time as possible is lost in reaching the necessary standard.

Freezer Compartments

These compartments must be thoroughly clean, dry and free from any odour or taint, and the surveyor must pay particular attention to the insulation, floor and any dunnage, to ensure there are no traces of any stain from a previous cargo.

The bilges must be inspected, and if necessary de-odourised, and the strum boxes free, and any valves on drain pipes must be freely working and closing tightly. After inspection the timber boards and tank manhole covers should be fitted into place, checked and then caulked or papered to provide a seal. The insulation must be thoroughly inspected, and any defect found, repaired, and any ventilator plugs wedged tightly in place, and sealed with sawdust. Should the compartment be in a tween deck — special care must be taken, when checking the scuppers, so as to ensure there is no possibility of taint odours rising from the bilges.

The dunnage to be used should be inspected, and must be clean and dry, and should be stowed in the freezer compartment before the compartment is cooled down.

The brine or air circuits must be tested, and the brine pipes should be tested to $1\frac{1}{2}$ times the normal working pressure, and then checked that there are no leaks, and that all fastenings and connections are secure.

After the compartments have been precooled, the surveyor should make a final check, that everything is in order and note the temperature, on each of the thermometers in the compartment.

It is usual for the compartments to be precooled to about the following temperatures:

Frozen goods	—	-10°C
Chilled goods	—	-5°F
Citrus fruits	—	-2°F
Other fruits	—	-1°F

This is usually a lower temperature than that at which the goods are to be carried, to compensate for an increase of temperature when loading.

Deeptank or Product Tanker Surveys

Before entering any tank it is imperative to ensure that it has been gas freed and tested, and that someone remains in attendance while he is in the tank. As an additional precaution, it is wise to have a self-contained breathing apparatus ready for use near the tank.

Double bottom tanks in the way of deep tanks must be pressure tested, usually to a head of 2 metres, and any defect rectified, and the deep tank itself is then pressure tested, though on occasions, the tanks are air tested at about 0.1 kg/cm^2, with the tank boundaries tested with a soapy solution. If the steam heating coils are to be used they should be tested with a steam pressure of 7 kg/cm^2, if they are not to be used, they should be removed and plugged.

The deep tank must be completely isolated, and the tank suction pipes blanked off at the bulkhead, the fire extinguisher pipes and the tank ventilators blanked off, and the sounding pipe extensions removed.

The tanks must be well cleaned, and this becomes very important, if the cargoes are edible oils, latex or wine. All rust, bituminous or metallic paint must be removed and after all residue has been removed, the tanks are steam cleaned, and then as soon as the lids are removed, washed down with water under pressure. After this the tanks are scrubbed with a hot caustic solution, and washed down again. The tank is then dried, and if the surveyor is satisfied, the tank is coated with the oil the tank is to carry, or waxed if the cargo is latex. Before allowing the tank to be waxed, the surveyor must also check that all brass, copper and galvanised fittings have been removed, and that special ventilation with relief valves have been properly fitted.

The cleaning of the tanks in a product tanker is usually easier, and though the same care must be exercised in checking them for cleanliness, it will be the pipes and valves used in loading and discharge that will cause the problem. Experience has shown that the majority of cases where contamination has occurred is due to dirty lines and/or valves, and it is sometimes necessary to have a valve dismantled to get it properly clean.

Surveying Dangerous Goods

The surveyor should see the dangerous goods before they are stowed, especially if they are being loaded into a container, so that he can check that the packaging complies with the regulations, and that the goods have been properly marked, and labelled, not only with the trade name, but also the correct technical name. He should also check that the notification of the intent to ship dangerous goods has been lodged with the Department of Transport (or appropriate authority).

He should examine the proposed stowage plan, to ensure that the 'blue' book regulations are complied with, and that poisonous and toxic goods are not to be stowed near foodstuffs, and to minimise the possibility of toxic or inflammable gases entering shipboard accommodation. It is just as important to check that the stowage has in fact, been carried out to plan, and that the goods are stowed securely, but this factor is sometimes forgotten.

Additionally, with containers, he should check that the dangerous goods are stowed so as to permit immediate access through the doors, and that goods requiring "away from" segregation are not stowed in the same container. He must also see that the container packing note is completed and placed in position.

Surveying a Timber Deck Cargo

The cargo must be stowed in accordance with the Deck Cargo Regulations, but the most important aspects to be looked for by the surveyor are:

(i)   that there has not been excessive loading of the deck, and the ship will retain adequate stability at all stages of the voyage.

(ii)   The timber should be stowed over the full available length, and that it does not interfere with the navigation or safe working of the ship, and doesn't prevent access to accommodation or steering gear, or impair ventilation.

(iii)   The stow in a well must be solid, and in a winter zone the maximum height of the stow is no more than one third of the extreme breadth of the ship.

(iv)   The cargo must be lashed, using as lashings, chain of a minimum size of 19mm, of FSWR of equivalent strength, with a sliphook and turnbuckle accessible at all times. The maximum distance apart of the lashings is 3 metres, and the eyeplate for the lashings must be attached to sheer-strake, and if necessary uprights are to be arranged along the ship's side. The first lashing must not be more than 2 metres from the adjacent bulkhead, and where there is no bulkhead, there must be lashings at 0.6 metres and 1.5 metres from the end of the stow.

(v)   Where a walkway must be built to give access to spaces used in working the ship, it must be at least a metre wide, with stanchions at a maximum spacing of 1.5 metres, and horizontal wires. The opening below the lowest wire must not exceed 230 mm, and the higher openings should not exceed 380 mm.

Grain Surveys

All ships loading a grain cargo must comply with various statutory regulations which are basically in two parts, requiring;

(1)   that the holds are in a clean and fit state to carry the cargo and

(2)   that the vessel's stability is adequate for the proposed loading and intended voyage.

In addition to the statutory requirements most Charter Parties will contain a clause, concerning surveys, and the one in the Australian Grain Charter, 1972, reads as follows:

> "Before loading is commenced the vessel shall pass the customary survey of a Commonwealth Department of Shipping and Transport Marine Surveyor, a Marine Underwriters Association Surveyor, a Lloyd's Register Surveyor, or other certified Surveyor approved by the Charterers."

Document of Authorisation and Certificate of Loading

Before grain can be loaded in bulk, the Master of each vessel must have a document of authorisation issued in accordance with;

      (a) Regulation 10, Part A of the Annexe to IMCO resolution A264 (iii)

or (b) Document CFR 144, 20-32, or the Navigation and Vessel's Inspection circular No. 10-69.

In addition the ship must have been inspected and passed free of infestation of any kind.

Before sailing, the Master of each vessel that has loaded grain in bulk, must have a certificate of loading (which is issued by an organisation recognised for that purpose). Such a certificate is prima facie evidence of compliance with the Grain regulations.

It should be noted that the certificate can not be issued if the ship has a list in excess of one degree, and becomes null and void if at any stage of the voyage the vessel is loaded over her seasonal marks. No allowance may be made for any residual ballast, that may be pumped out after the vessel's departure from the berth, or for hog or sag, and the vessel should have sufficient fuel and water to stay within a seasonal zone, should any deviation be necessary.

If the vessel is trimmed by the head on completion of loading, the Master must furnish a written statement to the affect that he considers it safe for the vessel to proceed to its destination in this condition. Where the stowage plan indicates slack or empty holds, it is the Master's responsibility to ensure that the longitudenal strength is not impaired.

Infestation

Although the standard of cleanliness and pest control is usually the responsibility of an officer of the Department of Primary Industry, the surveyor should be aware of the Regulations (in Australia these are the Export (Grain) Regulations made under the Customs Act 1901) and the standards required are continually being reviewed.

Inspections may only be made from half an hour after sunrise to half an hour before sunset, except in areas, such as store rooms, which are wholly or partially lit by artificial light where some relaxation of the time limit is permitted. Basically holds in which grain is to loaded must be free of live insects and rodents, and all parts of the hold must be substantially free from any cargo residue which is infestible by pests. The hold must be dry and free of any odour which might affect the grain loaded into them. Holds in which grain is not to be loaded, deck houses and storerooms, must not present a risk of cross infestation or contamination, and if such a risk is present, the Grain Loading Permit is withheld until the risk has been removed.

Should the holds or other areas require spraying or fogging, there are various insecticides and rodenticides recommended. After a spraying or fogging treatment, the inspection will be repeated, and a further spraying or fogging may be required if any insects or mites have survived.

Exemptions

If a ship has been exempted from any part of the 1969 Equivalent arrangement, a brief statement to this effect must be made on the first stage of the stability calculation form, and documentary proof must be shown to the surveyor at the port of loading.

If the distance from the edge of the coaming to either bulkhead is more than 2.4 metres, the ends must be trimmed unless dispensation has been granted by the state registering the ship, and an entry of heeling moments for 'filled' holds with untrimmed ends, are included in the Grain Loading Stability booklet, and taken into account in the calculation of the vessel's stability.

Where the saddle tanks slope at an angle of 30° or more, under the provisions of Part B, Section 1(A), (a) (ii), of the 1969 equivalent arrangement, trimming is not required in the hatch wings. If, however, the slope is less than 30°, and the distance from the coaming to the ship's side is greater than 2.4 metres, trimming will be required.

Forms

Each ship must fill in a form showing the calculation of stability required by the regulations it is intended to load under. The forms are reasonably straightforward but a few notes and formulae may help.

Ships loading under Chapter VI of the International Convention for the Safety of Life at sea 1960, are required to calculate the G.M. at departure and in the worst condition, and the angle of heel must be calculated for those specially constructed vessels to which Regulation 12 applies, e.g. bulk carriers. Loss of G.M. due to free grain in a feeder where shifting boards are not fitted can be found by the following:

$$\text{Loss of G.M.} = \frac{\text{Feeder length} \times (\text{Feeder breadth})^3}{6 \times \text{Stowage Factor} \times \text{Loaded Displacement}}$$

Note: foot ton units must be used

$$\text{Free surface correction} = \frac{\text{Free surface inertia moment}}{\text{Displacement}}$$

If insufficient data is available, upsetting moments for a compartment can be calculated from the formula

$$\text{Upsetting moment} = \frac{0.018 \, L \, b^3}{P} \text{ for a } 12° \text{ shift}$$

or

$$\text{Upsetting moment} = \frac{0.012 L \, b^3}{P} \text{ for a } 8° \text{ shift}$$

Note: foot/ton units must be used
in accordance with the requirements of Regulation 12 where
   L is the length of the upsetting wedge
   b is the breadth of the hold or hatchway taken at the free surface of the grain, allowing 2% sinkage

P is the stowage factor of the grain.

$$\text{Tangent Angle of Heel} = \frac{\text{Sum of upsetting moments}}{\text{G.M.} \times \text{Displacement}}$$

Ships loading under the 1969 equivalent arrangement are required to calculate the minimum value of G.M., the maximum angle of heel due to a grain shift, and the residual dynamic stability when heeled to 40°.

Under these regulations:
The minimum G.M. is to be not less than 0.30 metres, and the maximum angle of heel is 12°, and the required GZ at 40° heel is either 1.008 ft. or 0.307 metres.

When calculating the angle of heel, the unsecured grain surfaces are taken to repose at an angle of 15° to the horizontal in the voids below the hatch covers, and the deckhead area, and 25° to the horizontal in slack holds or tanks. Grain surfaces which have been secured by suitable cargo or strapped are considered not to shift, and therefore have no upsetting moments.

In the tables upsetting moments are usually given in volumetric units, and must be divided by the stowage factor to obtain foot/tons, or metre/tonnes. Occasionally tables will be found where the units are mixed, and care must be taken in these cases.

When calculating the GZ at 40°, the GZ obtained from the cross curves of stability, corrected for any K.G. difference must be reduced by the total upsetting arm of 40° heel. The upsetting arm is the sum of both its vertical and horizontal components, unless volumetric centres are being used when there is only a horizontal component. (The volumetric centre of a cargo compartment is the centre of gravity of the actual space.) Since cargo cannot be loaded to fill every part of that space, the volumetric centre must be higher than the centre of gravity in that space. When there is a shift in the surface of the grain there is a rise in the centre of gravity of the cargo below that surface. Up to 40° heel however, no matter how much the rise is, the centre of gravity of the cargo can never reach the height of the volumetric centre, and the vertical component is thus eliminated, as an allowance in excess of its value has already been used.

Horizontal component at 40° heel = 0.8 x upsetting arm for the vessel upright

Upsetting arm for the vessel upright = GM tan angle of heel (obtained from upsetting moments)

The vertical component Factor $\boxed{C}$ is usually obtained from the tables, but where this is not so, must be calculated from the formula

$$\text{Factor } \boxed{C} = \frac{0.08843}{\text{Displacement}} \times \text{sum of upsetting moments in all full}$$

$$\text{compartments} + \frac{0.15389}{\text{Displacement}} \times \text{sum of upsetting moments in all slack holds and tanks.}$$

Residual dynamic stability can be expressed in terms of the area below the fully corrected GZ curve. This area is enclosed by the curve and the horizontal axis, from the angle of heel due to grain shift through to 40°, and is calculated by using Simpson's Rules. The area thus found must not be less than 14.104 foot degrees, or 4.296 metre degrees.

The 40° upper limit, for calculating the area, is reduced; to
  (a) The highest point of the plotted curve, if this occurs before 40° heel
or (b) The ship's flooding angle, if this occurs before 40° heel.
      Note: Although the upper limit for calculating the area is reduced the curve must still be plotted to 40° heel.

The flooding angle (øf) is defined as that angle of heel, at which progressive flooding can occur, and applies to ships which have openings which permit this.

This curve must be plotted, and the area calculated in all cases where either:
  (a) the maximum corrected righting arm occurs before 40° heel, in the curves for the nearest typical loaded condition in the ship's Stability Booklet.
  (b) the slope of the curves indicate they would probably not contain the triangle contained, from 12° to 40° heel and to 1.008 ft. or 0.307 m.
  (c) the flooding angle of the ship is less than 40°
  (d) the calculated value of the corrected righting arm at 40° heel is critically close to the minimum of 1.008 ft. or 0.307 m.

Precautions when Loading

All compartments must be well trimmed, and loaded as fully as possible. In order to ensure this, the surveyor should, towards the completion of loading of the compartment, frequently sight the cargo through the trimming hatches and access manholes. It may sometimes be necessary to stop the loading and allow the dust to settle, in order to make a thorough check.

Weatherdeck Hatches

Sealing of the joints by tape is recommended, in order to prevent leakage through the metal joints; which may occur when the vessel is working in bad weather.

Stowage Factor

$$\text{Stowage Factor} = \frac{2240}{\text{Test weight}} \times 1.2445 \text{ ft.}^3/\text{ton}$$

The test weight is the actual weight in pounds of a U.S. bushel of the grain in question.

One U.S. bushel = 1.2445 ft.^{3}

Angles of Repose

Barley	46°	Rye	32°
Corn	21	Sunflower Seed	28
Linseed	21	Sorghum	31
Oats	21	Soya Bean	22
Rice	20	Wheat	23

DEPARTMENT OF TRANSPORT

**CALCULATION OF STABILITY
FOR A GRAIN SHIP LOADING
TO THE 1969
EQUIVALENT ARRANGEMENT**

Bulk Carrier	Tanker	T.Decker

S.S.
M.V.

Port Reg.

O.N.

Loading Ports

Discharge Ports

Cargo Plan: Indicate Holds, T'Decks, Eng. room, Cargo, Feeders, Trunks, Secured and unsecured gr surfaces.

State any exemptions from the 1969 equivalent arrangement: ....

....

....

I certify that the caulations shown in this document indicate values which will be maintained for this vess throughout the voyage.

....	....	....
Date	Port	Master

This form is to be completed for all vessels loading bulk grain under the 1969 equivalent arrangement less stabili data is submitted as prescribed by the Government of the vessel's country of registry.

ABLE 1. Calculation of KG by:-

(1) Cargo centres					(11) Volumetric centres (when used)		
Compart. No.	Worst condition with ballast if necessary				Indicate centre used		
	Weight		-KG	Moment	Centre	KG	Moment
Light Ship							
Crew at Stores							
					Total liquid moment from E		
Sub-Total					Grand Total of moments		
Tank No.					Free surface moment		
					F.S. Moment of Lube oil in stores		
Liquid Totals			E				
Grand Totals							

* When using computer complete weight and KG columns only
State name and serial number of computer

TABLE 1A Calculation of KG and GM

		(1)	(11)
Uncorrected KG from	$\dfrac{\text{Total Moments}}{\text{Displacement}}$	Ft M	Ft M
Liquid Free Surface Gain from	$\dfrac{\text{Total F.S. Moments}}{\text{Displacement}}$	+	+
Corrected KG for Cross Curves			OR
KM for Displacement Shown			
$\therefore$ Least GM = (Must not be less than 0.30 M)			

TABLE 2

(A) Upsetting Moments
(B) Vertical Component, Factor C
Not required when Volumetric Centres are being used

Com-partment No.	Grain Depth Ft/M	Stow-age Factor	Volumetric Upset Moments Ft⁴/M⁴	Upsetting Moments M/Kt	Factor C Ft/M
Totals					

TABLE 4. Corrected Righting Arm at 40 Heel using Cross Curves of Stability

	Ft M
GZ from C C's at 40°	
Corr. for KG Difference	
GZ Corrected for KG	
Total Upset. Arm at 40 Heel	
Corrected GZ at 40 Heel	
Required GZ at 40 Heel	1.008 Ft 0.307 M
Exceeds Minimum by –	

Hence Residual Area Exceeds Minimum Requirement of 14.104 Ft – Degrees
        4.296 M – Degrees

If the GZ Curve in the Nearest Typical Loaded Conditions is of Normal Form

TABLE 3.

(A) Angle of heel (B) Upsetting Arm at 40° Heel (C) Factor C Full Holds (D) Factor C Slack Holds/Trunks.
NOTE: The Factor C Sections are not required when Volumetric Centres are being used.

(A)
Tangent Angle of Heel = $\dfrac{\text{Total Upsetting Moments}}{\text{Displacement} \times \text{GM}}$ =   X   =
      Angle of Heel = _____ (Must not Exceed 12°)

(B)
Upsetting Arm for Vessel Upright = GM × Tan. Angle of Heel   =   ×   = A   Ft/M
Horizontal Component of Upsetting Arm at 40° Heel   = A × 0.8 = B   Ft/M
Vertical Component of Upsetting Arm at 40 Heel   = Factor C = C   Ft/M
$\therefore$ Total Upsetting Arm at 40° Heel   = B + C = D   Ft/M
NOTE: Value B is the Total Upset. Arm at 40° When Volumetric Centres are being used

(C) To Obtain a Value of That Part of Factor C for Deckhead Voids when not Given in the Stability Booklet.
Factor C = $\dfrac{0.08843}{\text{Displacement}}$ × (Sum of Upsetting moments in all Full Compartments)

     = 0.08843 $\left[\times \begin{array}{c}\text{F/Tons} \\ \text{M/Kt}\end{array}\right]$ =   Ft
                                           M

(D) That Part of Factor C for 25 Wedge shifts in Slack Holds and Trunks
Factor C = $\dfrac{0.15389}{\text{Displacement}}$ × (Sum of Upsetting moments in all Slack Holds and Trunks)

     = 0.15389 × $\left[\begin{array}{c}\text{F/Tons} \\ \text{M/Kt}\end{array}\right.$ Ft
                                           M

The upsetting arm curve is a straight line constructed from
the values in Table 5. Plot from Value A at 0° to Value B or D
at 40°. Measure ordinates for use in correcting the GZ values in Table 5.

TABLE 5. Correction of GZ values

Angles of Heel	5°	10°	15°	20°	25°	30°	35°	40°
GZ Values from Cross Curves								
Corrections for Diff. of KG's								
1st Corrected GZ Values								
Upsetting Arm Ordinates								
Fully Corrected GZ Values								

TABLE 6.
Simpson's Product For Area

Selected Ordinate	S.M.	Product for Area
	1	
	4	
	2	
	4	
	2	
	4	
	1	
Sum of Product		

UPSETTING ARM AND FULLY CORRECTED G.Z. (SCALE)

Angles of Heel (Limiting Ordinate for the area is at 40°, Angle of max. GZ Value or Flooding Angle whichever is least).

Are Under Curve = Selected Interval / 3 = Sum of Products

= 3/3 = FT. DEGREES
= M DEGREES

14.104 FT. DEGREES
4.296 M. DEGREES [Minimum Requirement

FORMULAE

1) $D_1 = D \pm \dfrac{B}{2} \tan \emptyset$

2) $x = d_1 \dfrac{(Df \sim Da)}{LPP}$

3) $y = d_2 \dfrac{(Df \sim Da)}{LPP}$

4) $z = d_3 \dfrac{(Df \sim Da)}{LPP}$

5) $h = \dfrac{tl}{LPP}$

6) Vol. void space $= \frac{1}{2}$ base $\times$ height $\times$ length

7) Approx. sounding corr. for trim $= \dfrac{\text{Trim (cm)} \times \text{Tank length(m)}}{2 \times LPP}$

8) Quarter mean draft $= \dfrac{DF + DA + 6\,DM}{8}$

9) Quarter mean draft $= DM \pm \frac{1}{4}\,(DM - DFA)$

10) $d = TPC - \dfrac{4 \times MTC}{LPP}$

11) Trim corr. $= \dfrac{TPC \times Trim \times 100}{LPP} \times dC + \left[\dfrac{50 \times dM \times Trim^2}{dZ}\right]$

12) Trim corr. $= \dfrac{TPI \times Trim \times 12}{LPP} \times dC + \left[\dfrac{6 \times dM \times Trim^2}{dZ}\right]$

13) $\dfrac{dM}{dZ} = ITM_1 - ITM_2$

14) $\dfrac{dM}{dZ} = \dfrac{30(TPI^2 - TPI^2)}{B}$

15) $\dfrac{dM}{dZ} = \dfrac{7.2\,(TPC^2 - TPC^2)}{B}$

16) Approx. List corr. $= 6\,(TPC_1 - TPC_2) \times (Dm_1 - Dm_2)$

17) Density corr. $= \dfrac{\text{Displacement} \times (1025 - \text{Observed density})}{1025}$

18) Corrected Displacement = $\dfrac{\text{Displacement} \times \text{Observed density}}{1025}$

19) Long Tons = $\dfrac{\text{Metric Tons}}{1.016047}$

20) Metric Tons = Long Tons $\times$ 1.016047

21) Feet = Metres $\times$ 3.2808

22) Metres = $\dfrac{\text{Feet}}{3.2808}$

23) Mass = Volume $\times$ density

24) Dts = Dto $\times$ CF $\times$ (ts–to)

25) Dt = $\dfrac{(W_2 - W_1) + C}{Wt_1}$

26) Metric tons = $\dfrac{\text{VTO} \times \text{VCF dts}}{1000}$

27) Long tons = $\dfrac{\text{Vto} \times \text{VCF} \times \text{dts}}{224}$

28) Quantity loaded = V (SG + WE) $\times$ (1 – VR)

29) Temporary working pressure elongation =
$\dfrac{\text{Lw} - \text{Lo} \times 100\%}{\text{Lo}}$

30) Permanent elongation = $\dfrac{\text{Lp} - \text{Lo} \times 100\%}{\text{Lo}}$

31) Degree of Loss = $\dfrac{\text{Sound Value} - \text{Damaged Value}}{\text{Sound Value}} \times 100\%$

32) Loss of GM = $\dfrac{\text{Feeder length} \times (\text{Feeder breadth})^3}{6 \times \text{Stowage Factor} \times \text{Loaded Displacement}}$

33) Free surface correction = $\dfrac{\text{Free surface inertia moment}}{\text{Displacement}}$

34) Upsetting moment 12^0 shift = $\dfrac{0.018\ L\ b^3}{P}$

35) Upsetting moment 8^0 shift = $\dfrac{0.012\ L\ b^3}{P}$

36) Tangent Angle of heel = $\dfrac{\text{Sum of upsetting moments}}{\text{GM} \times \text{Displacement}}$

37) Upsetting arm for vessel upright = GM tan. angle of heel

38) Horizontal component at 40^0 heel = 0.8 × upsetting arm for the vessel upright

39) Factor C = $\dfrac{0.08843}{\text{Displacement}}$ × sum of upsetting moments in all full compartments + $\dfrac{0.15389}{\text{Displacement}}$ × sum of upsetting moments in all slack holds and trunks

40) Stowage Factor = $\dfrac{2240}{\text{Test weight}}$ × 1.2445

SPECIFIC GRAVITY OF FRESH WATER

Temperature C	F	Specific Gravity	Volume in cubic cm. of one gram
0	32.0	0.99987	1.00013
4	39.2	1.00000	1.00000
8	46.4	0.99988	1.00012
12	53.6	0.99952	1.00048
16	60.8	0.99897	1.00103
20	68.0	0.99823	1.00177
24	75.2	0.99732	1.00268
28	82.4	0.99626	1.00374
32	89.6	0.99509	1.00495